Who Stole My Power?

And The Easy Way To Reclaim It!

Who Stole My Power?

And The Easy Way to Reclaim It!

By Felicity Okolo

Dynamic Life Coach & Speaker

http://www.felicityokolo.com

London

Email: felicity@felicityokolo.com

Knowing others is intelligence; knowing yourself is true wisdom. Mastering others is strength, mastering yourself is true power.

~ Lao-Tzu

ISBN: 978-1-4461-6284-2

This book is dedicated to my mother Helen Okolo who raised me to be the person I am today.

Acknowledgments

My sincere gratitude goes to the people who made this book possible. They are Elena Borissova, Raja Hireker, and Rev. Fr Casmir Dike for their encouragement and believe in me and for taking the time to read the first draft of the book. I would also like to thank Sunamita Lim for her help in research and my son, Jubilant, for his help with manuscript preparation.

My special thanks goes to my husband and children for their support and encouragement throughout the stages of this book development, my wonderful team of editors and designers, my mastermind group: Frank Lee, Joni Dunn, Vanessa Pacheco, Shelley Osterried and Sussana Huse, my seminar attendees and friends for their help and my Auntie Kate Ugochukwu for her everlasting support.

I love you all.

TABLE OF CONTENTS

INTRODUCTION 1

Chapter 1. LIFE AREAS 3

Chapter 2. SIX HUMAN NEEDS 41

Chapter 3. THREE HUMAN DESIRES TO EMBRACE-LOVE, HEALTH & WEALTH 57

Chapter 4. THREE HUMAN LIMITATIONS TO OVERCOME – F.E.A.R or (FALSE EVIDENCE APPEARING REAL) DOUBT & INSECURITY 65

Chapter 5. PERSONAL DEVELOPMENT APPLICATIONS 73

Chapter 6. SYSTEMIC IMPACT OF BELIEFS, VALUES & RULES 81

Chapter 7. LIVING AS SPIRITUAL BEINGS BY USING OUR INTUITION 85

References 97

About The Author 99

I hope our wisdom will grow with our power, and teach us that the less we use our power the greater it will be.
~ Thomas Jefferson

INTRODUCTION

What I find powerful is a person with the confidence to be her own self.

~ Oprah Winfrey

Millions around the world thrill to watching Oprah's inspiring TV shows. Why's that? The secret is simple—Oprah and her guests engage, educate and empower with illumining insights. 45 minutes of airtime with refreshingly positive people can boost a person's determination to overcome odds, and be in charge of his or her life and to keep on growing personally and professionally.

When you see other people shining forth their best qualities, bolstered by the fact that they've had to overcome their own perceived limitations in order to succeed, it means that you, too, can make it big time!

Oprah Winfrey is not your typical story of rags to riches and fame. But, it does show what's possible when *you* apply self-transcendence to overcome the odds. It also shows a deep knowledge and understanding of self in figuring out what it takes for a person to overcome hurdles to continue growing and succeeding with their life. You and I may not be Oprah or the other famous people mentioned in this book but we all have the same potentials and gifts as them. I have written this book to encourage you to reach within you and see your true potentials and gifts waiting for you to bring forth and shine for yourself and the highest good of everyone.

Follow me and embark on a personal journey of uncommon self-discoveries, and become a hero on life's battlefield that you didn't think possible before!

That's the way life is meant to be lived and enjoyed—with confidence, honest appreciation of self and others and utilising one's potential power from within to transform challenging outer circumstances into win-win-win and successful outcomes.

So, you might ask, why is this simple and powerful secret so well hidden from the rest of us? Let me share with you the story of, *The Littlest God.*

It wasn't long after the Gods had created humankind that they began to realize their mistake. The creatures they had created were so adept, so skillful, so full of curiosity and the spirit of enquiry that it was only a matter of time before they would start to challenge the Gods themselves for supremacy.

To ensure their pre-eminence, the Gods held a large conference to discuss this issue. Gods were summoned from all over the known and unknown worlds. The debates were long, detailed, and soul-searching.

All the Gods were very clear about one thing. The difference between them and the mortals was the difference between the quality of the resources they had. While humans had their egos and were concerned with the external, material aspects of the world, the Gods had spirit soul, and an understanding of the workings of the inner self.

The danger was that sooner or later the humans would want some of that inner wealth, too.

The Gods decided to hide their precious resources. The question was: where? This was the reason for the lengthy and passionate debates at the Great Conference of the Gods.

Some suggested hiding these resources at the top of the mountain. But it was realized that sooner or later, any human being could scale such a mountain.

And the deepest crater in the deepest ocean would be discovered.

And mines would be sunk into the earth.

And the most impenetrable jungles would give up their secrets.

And mechanical birds would explore the sky and space.

And the moon and the planets would become tourist destinations.

And even the wisest and most creative of the Gods fell silent as if every avenue had been explored and found wanting. Then…

Chapter 1.

LIFE AREAS

To know yourself is to realise that you are more than the little self that has been given to you by your history—the pattern that others made—that your true self is, in truth, much larger and includes other people, other cultures, other species even. That life is less about being and more about inter-being. We come to know ourselves, then, through coming to know each other. And the deeper that knowledge, the richer and more creative the world we build together.

~ Danny Martin

Personal Development

Contrary to what the general perception may be, all areas of one's life cannot be separated. We may think that because we compartmentalise our activities into work, play, exercise or rest that our personal being is quite disparate. But in truth, these different areas of a person's life are unique to the individual and have to be treated with equal importance. This is *the* challenge—to integrate all the areas into a fully functioning and positive whole.

That's where the sum of our parts is greater than the whole. When every part is working together and synchronising beautifully, we sing the joy of living in harmony—as when an orchestra plays in perfect pitch and synchronicity. The ripple effects are felt when you (or the orchestra) impart your inimitable vibrations to others.

As Danny Martin's quote tries to explain, "*Your true self is, in truth, much larger and includes other people, other cultures, other species. We come to know ourselves, then, through coming to know each other.*"

Yes, that is the whole point—we need to understand ourselves first, before we can interact to the best of our abilities with other people.

The catch? No one can do it for you. *YOU have to want* to feel you're enriching your life with self-knowledge and to understand yourself by being motivated to doing it—because no one can do it for you! My book can encourage you with inspiring examples. I can cheer you on to getting started with simple techniques we'll be covering.

How many of us can really say we know and understand who we are? We're busy enough running helter-skelter raising a family, getting to work on time and paying bills—with precious little time for quiet time to delve deeper for insights into who we really are, how to cultivate our strengths, mitigate our weaknesses and to discover what our life's mission is.

Yet, it's paramount to know oneself. This process is called the intuitive art of personal development. It's important to ask:

What can I do to get to know me better through self-development?

What would happen if I didn't embrace the personal journey of self-development and self-discovery?

This is the central concept of my book—to help you discover your potential by developing awareness of your deeper, hidden self and in the process, to acquire a better understanding of ***who*** you truly are. When you understand what your Divinity means as a human being, from the very depths of your heart and soul, you play bigger and can transform yourself and the world with your sincere intentions.

We discover we are truly larger than the sum of our parts the moment we start our personal quest. We find out, too, how very interdependent we are on every part of our being. Each part has to be treated with equal importance. For example, we cannot enjoy a tasty meal with our mouths alone. We also need the food to be assimilated by the body's digestive system in order to provide nutrients to nourish the entire body. So, on it goes.

The potential of every human being is truly unlimited—if we dare, and look within. We're as capable as we think we are, or not. As Henry Ford pointed out, *"Whether you think you can or cannot, either way you are right."*

It's a classic case of seeing whether your glass is half-full or half-empty, a perception fostered by our social upbringing. Henry Ford also correctly noted that our lives and the world we live in are meant to develop and build character. He urged his factory workers to accept and deal with setbacks, plus face grief in the face of loss. Such events do in fact help personal growth, not only personally, but also in the collective march forward towards continued success for everyone.

And that is the paradox of life—to accept whom we are, to celebrate personal victories and to acknowledge losses—that's all part of mortal living. Life happens. And, we have to learn how to meet Life headlong!

That's where a keen knowledge and understanding of who we are, and what we're capable of doing, pays dividends in: 1) meeting 2) accepting and 3) dealing headlong with life's numerous challenges.

Especially when the only certainty in life is—CHANGE.

You'll notice how I've inserted "accepting" changes into the equation where **LIFE = meeting + accepting + dealing with challenges.**

That is because we're so often traumatised by negative events that we sweep them under the carpet, not realising that we need to *accept* them first, in order to transform them into positive opportunities.

Let's take Oprah Winfrey as an example. Sexually abused while growing up, these experiences made a vulnerable child withdraw from the world. However, Oprah found the answer out of her misery. She thrilled to the joy of spending hours enriching her senses by reading books.

Even in her darkest moments, Oprah's inner strength showed her that the world was hers to conquer. Perhaps it was the quiet times alone that gave her the chance to delve within to empower herself—and to emerge as a butterfly sharing her real beauty with other people, and showing us that, yes, we can find and pull out our inner Light, too.

She could, and did, pull herself out of emotional self-doubt to become the very epitome of a confident and successful entrepreneur. For years now, Oprah has been the wealthiest celebrity on the annual Forbes Celebrity 100 ranking.

In order to be HAPPY and SUCCESSFUL, you have to start by loving yourself. The reason why people feel lousy about themselves and fail to achieve their goals is—they don't like who they are.

Can you imagine not liking who you are? How preposterous!

Many people think they must first become successful according to some corporate definition before they can start loving themselves and enjoying their lives.

In fact, the opposite is true. **You must first love yourself**—before you can become successful. People who love and feel good about themselves have what's called, *high self-esteem.*

When you love yourself and have boundless confidence in who you are, what you're able to achieve and contribute back to the world—then you'll have discovered the most profound reason for living, by knowing who you are, and understanding what you're capable of doing and contributing for yourself, others and the world.

And, the way to realising your own high self-esteem is to acknowledge that you are of The Source - The Supreme Source that created everyone to reflect divine love, goodness, and beauty.

When we know the essence of who we are and of Whom we're from, then it makes it so much easier to love ourselves—even if others don't.

You may have wondered why you don't "click" with certain groups. Instead of plunging into self-doubt, insecurity and fear, when you know that you're of the Source, you'll be able to assert your self-esteem in *knowing* the value of your true worth—by moving on.

It's alright to move on and hang out with other people and groups who reflect your own aspirations. And, you gain even more confidence to know you have this awareness of Self. What is this "Self?" This is what we'll find out in this next section—when we aspire to our highest.

Spiritual Aspiration

> Aspiration is a glowing flame that secretly and sacredly uplifts our consciousness and finally liberates us. Unlike other flames, this flame does not burn anything. It purifies, illumines and transforms our life. Aspiration is our inner urge to transcend both the experience and the realisation already achieved.
>
> ~ Sri Chinmoy, in
>
> *The Divine Hero: Winning in the Battlefield of Life*
> (Watkins, 2002)

Oprah Winfrey openly speaks of her faith in God and the Universe. It's this deep inner faith of knowing who she is and what she's capable of doing and sharing with others that is so inspiring for her TV viewers and readers of *O, The Oprah Magazine*. It also speaks volumes that inner wealth, when acknowledged and honoured sincerely, does enrich a person's outer life and the lives of others, as well.

The problem with the traditional model has been putting the cart before the horse in chasing after outer material trappings before building a strong personal foundation. That is why you're reading this—to reverse that tendency by focusing on your self, first.

However, I'm not talking about being self-centred or selfish. Rather, for a change of pace, you're *getting to know your self* as never before—because it hasn't been a part of the socialisation process for most people.

You're striving to breathe naturally and to exhale the real in you. You're interested in finding out how you can make progress with your life, naturally—by nurturing your higher self to guide your outer persona.

To know oneself is indeed taking the first, right step. Yes, it's learning to build a relationship with *your* self first. We've all been socialised into building relationships with others, we forget we have to know who we are first—in order to know others. First things, first.

We need to know we've been labeled, stamped and brought up into believing who we are by outer forces of socialisation that also influence family environments. In other words, we've been left in the dark of what our true worth and value are—from inside. Of what our true potential talents are, and to allow them to shine forth in our lives, so we ultimately live a happy life by fulfilling our potential from within—not from other people's expectations of what we ought to be and how to act and behave from the outside.

The second step, after discovering and getting to know our true mental, is needing to understand what we can do with our lives in order to overcome and transcend these outer circumstances and other people's expectations.

Thus, TOTAL LIFE ENRICHMENT comes from:

1 **Knowing** how you can imprint *your own stamp* by shedding unreal outer beliefs that have been holding you back

2 **Understanding** your true worth and value to enable you to assert your inimitable personality and inner Light onto a perceived world stage; a public arena that beckons with artificial lights and moulding conventional expectations according to other people's needs and standards

In other words, you need to know and understand yourself first, before name, fame and professional recognition bestow their

trappings on you. It's imperative for personal development to effect changes in you first, so material gains do *not* define you.

And, it is this progress with one's spiritual seeking that provides the inner foundation for all outer success—be it running your own business, raising a family or working for a company.

Without a solid inner foundation to *love and appreciate what your real self-worth* is, it's very hard to live a happy and enriching life when you need to interact with others at work, at play and just about everywhere you turn to.

Why? Because you'll feel beholden to accept what others think of, and say about, you! While in fact, you have all the innate powers from within to demystify old societal norms that have been holding you back in terms of social behaviour and mannerisms—even as you need to imprint and assert *your* True Self to discover true joy in living your dreams.

That is what knowing and acknowledging your True Self does for you. It's quite a sea change when *you understand* what you can do, to empower your mind, to shut out withering comments that don't allow you to grow emotionally and professionally.

Of course, this doesn't imply breaking societal norms that preserve law and order. What it does mean, however, is you're on course to uncover your true spiritual potential to guide, protect and nourish your daily living on a solid footing.

You'll be liberated and free—to prevail on Your Own True Divinity as the real GPS (Global Positioning System) for lasting happiness, wherever you are!

Being spiritual may mean showing signs of outer devotion by going to church, synagogue, mosque or temple on a weekly basis or merely during the high holidays or contributing to religious fundraisers and church benefits.

But, most of all, being spiritual is a person's quiet introspection into the eternal 64-million dollar questions—"who am I?" and "whose am I?"

Avid outdoorsy types come close to discovering some answers to these important life-changing and life-enhancing questions. Mother Nature is the most natural extension of The Source. Hikers, campers and naturalists cannot help but soak in not only rain, but also gorgeous rainbows and clear blue skies softly dotted with wispy patches of cotton-candy clouds—to realise moments of inner Eureka!

Or, someone who has had a near-death experience; and recovered to be eternally grateful in living the Gift of Life as fully as possible at every moment.

Gratitude is a spiritual quality that we dearly need—yet many neglect to express this elemental vibration by offering it back to the Universe and to other people who have graced their lives.

Spirituality is:

1 First, acknowledging our inner core, our very foundation, as fundamental to developing and living a fulfilling life.

2 Second, because we're all different, to find our inner gems, each in our own way, by using different techniques—affirmations, visualisation, meditation and prayer or journaling for example—to access our inner wealth.

3 Third, to bring these gems up to the light and burnish them as best as possible, in order to reflect back to the outer world who we truly are. That is what character-building is all about—to know who we truly are and to aspire to be the very best we can be in everything that we do.

In a nutshell, **spiritual aspiration manifests your spirituality in very practical ways.** Such as, aspiring to be the very best you can be, with your God-blessed talents buried deep within—talents that are patiently waiting for you to unearth and shine for living a happier life.

That is why **personal development is a lifelong process of seeking** and discovering your highest from within—based on a deep spiritual foundation of knowing and understanding yourself first.

How does spiritual aspiration work? A singer aspires to be the best performer he or she can be—by having a goal and a dedicated action plan to practice daily in order to cultivate and hone their talent.

Creating and developing your life plan also means being flexible in tweaking your goals and expectations to match realistic gains. That is what my workshops, goal setting CD and personal coaching sessions do—to unearth your divine potential for satisfying personal and professional results. For further details on the above mentioned products and services visit www.felicityokolo.com.

We know, too, that success and victory do not appear at first blush. Instead, it means chipping away at honing and developing the divine gifts we're born with.

Personal development is an ongoing, lifelong process!

A real-life inspiring example is Marianne Williamson who, at age 26, was feeling lost and desperate after indulging in the excesses of the 1960s, wrote a book called *A Return to Love: Reflections on the Principles of "A Course in Miracles"*.

Marianne correctly points out, *"Our deepest fear is not that we are inadequate. Our deepest fear is that we are powerful beyond measure. It is our light, not our darkness that most frightens us. We ask ourselves, who am I to be brilliant, gorgeous, talented and fabulous? Actually, who are you not to be? You are a child of God—your playing small doesn't serve the world. There is nothing enlightened about shrinking so that other people will not feel insecure around you. We were born to make manifest the glory of God that is within us. It is not in just some of us; it is in everyone. And as we let our own light shine, we unconsciously give people permission to do the same. As we are liberated from our own fear, our presence automatically liberates others."*

I agree we're spiritual beings with more innate powers than we can ever use—yet we play small!

That is why I want you to look inward to discover what your unique treasures are. That is why this process is called self-discovery—to discover your personal strengths and mission in life, by taking a journey of personal development with me.

Like any journey of a thousand steps, we begin our inner seeking or spiritual search with the first step, such as with introspection, prayer and meditation. Practiced daily, these inner techniques grace an adventure-filled journey that transports, guides and illumines our outer actions.

Not only will you see positive results—your spouse, family, co-workers and friends will notice a new shine and a spring in your steps! And, like Marianne Williamson points out—your inner light and positive energy impact and liberate other people to look for their inner shine, too!

All you need to start by way of personal investment is to set aside 5-10 minutes in the morning. As the saying goes, morning shows the day. We've heard of development banks to grow economies. Invest in your personal development bank to grow your own potential. When you reflect inwardly, pray, say affirmations and meditate, you're consciously earning spiritual money to deposit into your inner bank or your heart bank that you can withdraw from, during the day.

Isn't accessing your inner potential a practical way to enrich your outer life? Plus, you're in total control—no therapists or head-shrinks need apply!

Then, during the course of the day, when you need peace in the midst of life's hustle-and-bustle, you can pull out "serenity-dollars" to remain poised and calm if your boss raises his or her voice at you. Or, you'll have more than enough inner wealth to follow your bliss in starting a new enterprise with innovative ideas and abundant energy.

That is how you start learning to play bigger than you've been doing—by enriching your outer self with solid personal growth in knowing and understanding what you're capable of doing—by accessing the Soul's priceless treasures.

The benefits of personal development and spiritual growth in getting to know your deeper self will gift you these positive results:

- Confidence to live your life as you enjoy it
- Happiness in going with your natural inclinations
- Increased energy to pursue more projects and to reap their rewards
- Harmony in living your life with peace of mind
- A loving heart of compassion and identification
- The ability to forgive yourself and others
- Letting go of stress before dis-ease sets in
- The sincere aspiration to keep challenging yourself on to higher heights of achievements
- Aspiration is also a spiritual metaphor that purifies and illumines your mental and physical energies. How? It works like a candle. When you aspire, you're determined to access only the best from within; in doing so, your highest and best qualities emerge to purify, illumine and transform your lesser qualities. That is what a candle does, too, in illumining a darkened room. You need to bring Light into your mind room. When your mind is purified by your Soul's light, it works magic by being mentally focused and crystal clear in doing right by you!
- To live a positive life that attracts abundance and prosperity in never wanting or settling for less

- ❖ The ability to live a more fulfilling and satisfying life
- ❖ To share and give to others unconditionally, even as more good things come your way—as in what goes around, comes around
- ❖ To keep dreaming and living your dreams realistically and in very pragmatic ways

That is why **being spiritual is a natural part of living life fully**—and all the more reason to reconnect with your higher self to guide and direct your outer actions to enrich you exponentially.

These inclinations to be true to yourself have probably surfaced as you were walking along the beach or gardening in your yard. They happened because you were momentarily caught off guard by your inner being reaching out during quiet moments—which is harder when your day is filled with an active mind and lifestyle.

It's only when you're not running around trying to meet deadlines or catch the bus that you let down your guard—and allow the inner wellspring of Light to sparkle forth and inspire your thoughts and guide your natural inclinations.

Learn to listen to your intuition. It is the real language and meaningful communication from the depths of your soul to your outer mind as you try to figure out what to do. The mind is totally fickle and changing it's course all the time. However, the light of your soul will shine a true course of action every time.

Here are some methods to access and build up your foundation for personal development, starting with meditation—evidence that peaceful meditation can fuel dynamic living with this exercise.

Starting off with even one minute pays amazing dividends. Before you know it, you'll miss saying hello to your meditation friend if you forget to tune in for your energy picker-upper at a regular time—say around 3 p.m. when your energy reserves need a daily boost.

Learning to Meditate

1. **Sit comfortably on a straight-backed chair. Loosen your clothing so you're comfy and at ease.**
2. **Close your eyes if you like. Have your hands relaxed in your lap.**
3. **Take a deep and invigorating breath, at your own pace—one, two.**
4. **Feel this new breath of fresh energy flowing into every pore of your being—three, four. Exhale stale energy from your body—five, six.**
5. **Keep repeating until you feel energised, purified and cleansed with new energy that is revitalising your entire being.**
6. **Your rewards? More dynamic energy and less calories because it beats reaching out for that Cadbury bar, anytime and every time!**

Another personal development tool that provides lots of inner assurances and confidence for everyone is prayer. Have you caught yourself exclaiming, "Thank God, I stopped turning round the corner before that crazy driver hit me!?@!#" This is prayer at its most utilitarian form—expressing thanks to the Universe while releasing acute anger.

Prayers are also offered for loved ones to compete successfully for jobs, school examinations and even for a birthday cake to turn out good! When we pray, we invoke yet another form of subtle energy. It's subtle energy that heals emotionally, mentally and physically.

Prayer and meditation are invisible energy forms that connect us from within to without, with other people and to the environment. Acknowledging how important they are, while being free for the taking, is a first step to recognising the importance of inviting spiritual aspiration to enrich our lives.

It's interesting to see how prayer works as an outgoing energy movement as you ask a higher power to help you, while meditation is an inward-turning process to still the mind to receive these answers from The Source. These messages come from the light of your soul via your intuition and voice of conscience.

Both prayer (talking to a Higher Power) and meditation (listening to Divinity's answers springing up from the depths of our souls) are complementary and necessary for personal discovery. We're so used to voicing our thoughts, intentions and invocations out loud; we forget that learning to listen is important, too. Listening is an art.

Listening in this case means—learning to listen to your Self.

Two other practical spiritual techniques are: affirmation and visualisation. An affirmation is a purposeful phrase or sentence that you repeat to affirm and confirm your intentions. It's a mantra or powerful sacred repetition of a divine intention for positive results. Your sincere intentions fuel the powerful forces that make your wishes come true.

The body-mind-soul connection is palpably powerful, especially when you visualise your goals to envision tangible results.

Applying Affirmation & Visualisation to Daily Living

1. **With help from your daily meditations, intuitively seek what you need to rebalance your life with, by seeking and invoking aspirations that are spiritually-based—more energy, happiness, or even a job promotion.**
2. **Write down, for example "I am the new project manager for our XYZ campaign for workplace healthy eating and exercise," if that is your professional goal to getting ahead at work. Or, "I'm going to lose 5 pounds in 10 days," for a personal goal.**
3. **Notice how you have to be focused on your goal, with details thrown in for tangible outcomes.**
4. **Say it out loud, softly; repeat as often as you like. [Tip: great for drive times during your commute or while taking the subway.]**
5. **Most important point—an affirmation is only powerful when you repeat it sincerely and convincingly to your mind and body.**
6. **Be sure to clearly see that it's happening in your mind's eye. That is envisioning success to happen.**

There are three simple techniques that are the foundation stones in growing your spiritual awareness for personal development:

1 Prayer for divine intervention—for protection, assistance and expressing unequivocal gratitude back to the Universe for the blessings you receive.

2 Meditation for peaceful and dynamic living. When you allow your Soul's answers to be heard by your entire being, from your mind to your body and vital, it's an amazing transformative experience. When this happens, Life's synchronicity starts unifying daily living into a song of coherent oneness—when you're happy and willing to do what's right, without the mind coming in to contradict your actions nor your vital unwilling to contribute readily.

3 Affirmation and visualisation to harness your potential in connecting your soul's light with your mental intentions and physical actions.

If you're a parent, you'll be gratified when your children look back and thank you for sharing these simple secrets in getting ahead with their personal growth. In turn, they'll likewise do the same for their kids—just like expanding on a house that is already built on a solid foundation—with ongoing positive ramifications for future generations.

If you've never tried these techniques before, it's never too late to reconnect with the highest part of yourself, with the Light from within. The drive to grow from within hits us at various times in life. Just be thankful that you're now at the stage where you're able to inquire into making progress from within. Opportunity always presents itself when time is opportune and the outer being is ready to act.

Money & Outer Wealth

Often, when we hear the phrase, "giving back," we automatically think of contributing to charities with money and/or our time and expertise.

However, it's just as important to give back whole-heartedly to people and organisations you work for. At the most fundamental level, short of receiving an inheritance, this is how you accrue the ability to pay bills on time and in the process, grow outer wealth.

That is why I'm emphasising the importance of giving back as much as you can to your employer. It's a mutual win-win for both sides. When your heart is in what you do, it shows. At a time when jobless rates are soaring, have you stopped to offer gratitude to your employer? It's spiritual aspiration at work, in the workplace.

Work joyfully and peacefully, knowing that right thoughts and right efforts will inevitably bring about right results.

~ James Allen

Now, I'm going to help you actualise outer wealth with the Law of Attraction. You may have heard of *The Secret*, an amazing book and movie of the same title that came out in 2004 authored by Rhonda Byrne. We can learn lots from this author to grow and actualize our financial dreams.

Rhonda was a down-and-out mother who happened to stumble on "the secret" of self-discovery by using the law of attraction. At the time of her breakthrough, she had recently lost her father and was facing less than positive relationships with her family and co-workers. She had been slowly loosing her grip on reality as her downward spiral progressed.

Journalist and author Karen Kelly wrote in her book, *The Secret of "The Secret"* (St. Martin's Press, 2007), that Rhonda's daughter Hayley gave her mother a one-hundred-year old book describing "the secret" which was, *The Science of Getting Rich*, written by Wallace Wattles in 1910.

Wattles explained that like attracts like. Quantum physicists also talk about the laws of energy where like attracts like, based on similar vibrations called frequencies that are given out and received, and that are transmitted all over again to like-minded channels.

Therefore, when you articulate and emit positive thoughts to bring about abundance to your life, then you would attract equally similar vibrations that will keep you in financial straights forever. So, too, in imagining good thoughts such as health and other goodies like honest relationships.

But, if you harboured negative worries such as struggling to pay rent and haunted by the fear of poverty, then you would attract similar vibes to stake you in tight financial straits, forever.

The beauty of the Law of Attraction is that you can always shift your thoughts from negative to positive—and start afresh in attracting health, wealth and love - any time you're committed to changing your life course with positive self-discovery.

Rhonda discovered that the greatest people in history had used the Law of Attraction to their advantage—Plato, Shakespeare, Newton, Beethoven, Lincoln, Emerson and Einstein to name a few.

Regardless of what it's called—the power of positive thinking, the power of deliberate intention, and the flow of abundance, neuropsychology or affective neuroscience—when you sincerely offer intense energy and vibrations to the Universe for help in any field, you will be heard and you will be helped!

Yes, you *can* help yourself to prosperity, good health and love! You only have to *want to start* and faithfully offer your positive intentions daily. The challenge is to get started. It's also true that the rewards are motivations that encourage you to continue doing them whenever you feel inspired to, every day.

That is why I'm including daily rituals and practices to get you started on a good habit that reinforces itself. Begin with these three simple and easy steps outlined in the TO DO box below.

TO DO: DAILY INTENTIONS

1. **Offer *Prayers* of Gratitude for the Gift of tuning in to your abundant Self-Awareness. Start the day with five minutes of sincere prayers to guide, protect and nurture your day's abundant activities yet to come.**
2. **Offer five minutes of silent** *meditation* **to "listen" to your Soul's light for intuitive guidance. Even if no answers are forthcoming, proceed with the abiding Faith that the answers will spring forth intuitively when you need them. Divine Time is quite different from the mind's calculating timelines and schedules.**
3. **Offer two minutes of** *intense affirmations* **where you sincerely focus on the intent(s) you're invoking. For instance, you'd like to start paying bills on time. Imagine yourself writing out payments for the actual amounts due. See the money coming into your bank account to pay your bills. No hesitation, no waffling—just pure faith that money arrives on time. And, the miracle of your deep faith always ensures that it does!**

Affirmations are powerful when loaded with specific and positive intentions, as you learned above, by repeating them and conducting strong mind-body connections to actualise tangible results.

Think about it. It's very powerful and liberating to empower yourself with the basic tools to fulfil as many accomplishments as you wish. Wishing upon a star is easy, after all. And, in the process liberate and empower others, too, as Marianne Williamson points out.

Especially in a world filled with unpredictable events. For example, who had thought that buying houses as investments would backfire, even as recently as a few years ago? Now, many homeowners are facing foreclosures and are "under water" with homes worth lots less than what they had originally paid for.

Know that you *can* attract money and wealth. Money on its own is without power or energy. However, **you are a magnet** attracting to you all things you wish, via the signals you're emitting through your thoughts and feelings. That is how you attract money.

This is a secret that is easy to practice and attain. You only have to make time for a few minutes to invest in yourself and your aspirations to attract abundance. As older civilisations such as the Chinese and the Indians know, living a life of abundance means not wanting in any way.

That is how you, too, can envision money flowing into your wallets and purses—by being **a magnet for money with your energetic aspirations to build financial security**. The caveat though, is to ask for money to help yourself and your family—without thoughts of any wrongdoing from ill-gotten sources.

Money Mantra Magnet Exercise

- Imagine a specific amount of money you want to meet your needs.
- Write down the exact amount you want for each item.
- Write a precise affirmation: "I want £25,000 for my daughter's university tuition."
- Say aloud your money mantra or affirmation a few times daily.
- Say your mantra sincerely, without making demands on the Universe.
- Envision this affirmation as an honest attempt to help someone achieve their honest goals—in meeting your daughter's higher education goals to pay for her tuition.
- Thank the Universe for helping you.

Now, lest you think I'm advocating an irresponsible way to generate money without working for it, let me quickly assure you that positive affirmations only work because they are honest, used for positive gains and help people with personal development goals.

As President Franklin Delano Roosevelt said at his first inauguration, *"Happiness lies not in the mere possession of money; it lies in the joy of achievement, in the thrill of creative effort."*

That is the reason why billionaires continue creating wealth, for the pure joy of challenging themselves to grow and expand their financial goals and harvesting the rewards of achieving more, by trying innovative ways to grow money.

Creativity is another great personal development goal and process to seek. So, give yourself the benefit of innovating new and different ways of attracting money, as a positive money magnet force with all the right and positive intentions to benefit you and your family!

Quantum Energy Tips on How to Become a Money Magnet

As I'd mentioned earlier, the Law of Attraction is an energy force of like wavelengths attracting like vibrations. Just because we do not see energy, it doesn't mean we can't feel it—we do!

Here are some practical tips to developing your personal wavelengths in becoming a money magnet:

- ❖ Visualise your ability to attract financial rewards as a money magnet. Imagine the money is already on its way to you. (Don't spend it yet, though. ☺)
- ❖ Perceive and believe that you're achieving money success with the magnetic mindset of a financially independent individual. Delete negative thoughts of, "I can't afford it" or, "It's too much to spend."
- ❖ Say a sincere thank–you to the Universe for the money you already have. As I've said, Gratitude is another form of wealth—inner wealth on which outer wealth accrues.
- ❖ Cultivate a positive mindset that money comes to you easily and effortlessly (you still have to put in the sweat equity, though)
- ❖ Every time you catch a doubting thought that you're less than capable of attracting money, squash it as you would a bug! Remember, like generates like.
- ❖ Abundance is a positive vibration. Abundance means never ever feeling a lack in anything—starting with food and shelter for our basic needs and a good-fit job that is win-win for you and your employer. Since like attracts like, positive energies such as unconditional love, joy (follow your bliss!), serenity, beauty, confidence, humility, sincerity, purity and gratitude are magnets for money, finances, productive employment opportunities, too.

- ❖ Most of all, **love yourself**! If you cannot forgive yourself, go past disappointments, failures (remember, failures are the pillars of success) and anger, these negative energies will negate your positive aspirations!!

Money has no power of its own. You alone are the power source. Power comes from who you are, not what you have.

~ Suze Orman, "Money Lady"

Family and Influence

Nowhere is it more evident than in a family situation that no person is an island. The warmth of spoken or unspoken love, sharing good news, giving moral support when not-so-good news surfaces, or being there for each other promotes an understated and unconditional give-and-take that sustains body, mind, and spirit at every moment.

Family is where it all starts. Are you there for each other? Or do family members amble home at various times, heat up a microwave dinner, and retreat to their own bedrooms to eat and watch TV?

Parents own the important responsibility for how they bring up their children. Parenting that is caring, respectful and encouraging will impact children long after they leave home. Children take with them impressions and memories in how they were raised and use them when raising their own families. So the pattern goes on, generation after generation.

That is not to say everything is going to be rosy all the time. That is just not reality. Reality living, though, is when family members acknowledge problems and try to find workable solutions together, harmoniously, and with love in their hearts.

Note the word *harmony*. On the whole, when family members don't yell and fight like cats and dogs, you can see it in the children's eyes—eyes that are peaceful, poised, and self-assured, eyes that look you directly in your eyes. However, when kids shift their gazes away, you know something is not quite right. These are "trouble signs" to watch out for in your kids.

Take the time to show your love and attention to your children by spending time with them—at the dinner table, doing yard work, and volunteering for community causes.

Kids learn from watching—watching adults such as their parents, teachers, and TV's … uh … "role models." Who would you rather your kids emulate? If the obvious answers are staring at you in the face, you'll obviously need to develop your own personal graces first.

Every family has its own sets of unique interactions among members, its own give-and-take by different persons at various times. There is a hidden order in family dynamics that is similar to the inborn intelligence imprinted in the human body. The microcosm of dynamic interactions balance out with the underlying power of love in the family unit.

For example, there are good days and not-so-good days. If issues need resolving, you keep the dialogue going for the next few days until solutions present themselves. There is constant back-and-forth. Outsiders may not understand; they may even label it dysfunctional, but the healing power of love ultimately unites the family as a coherent unit.

President Barack Obama, the first African-American president voted into a democratic presidency, is conscious of how he and his wife's actions impact their kids. These two busy world leaders and parents of now eleven-year-old Malia and eight-year-old Sasha know how important it is to be inspiring family role models.

Michelle Obama told *Children's Health* magazine in the November 2009 issue that like most parents, she and the President are too busy to think about staying fit and healthy every day. "But health and fitness and how we eat and thinking about it has become part of our lives, because of our kids. We are their primary role models. And if they see me exercising and thinking about what I'm eating, if they see their father, as busy as he is, getting to the gym and playing sports, when they grow up they'll understand that this is a natural part of being an adult."

The First Lady of the United States also shared smaller changes to the family's diet that have made a lasting difference—avoiding processed foods, cutting back on sugary drinks, eating more fresh fruits and vegetables (including starting the world-famous White House garden with an elementary school—what a great idea!), eating together as a family, and teaching her daughters how to read food labels.

When your kids look back on how you nurtured them by taking small steps that made a huge difference in building a strong and healthy lifestyle, they'll be forever grateful to you!

An ounce of prevention is worth pounds of cure later—physically, emotionally, mentally, and spiritually—as you lay the best and most solid foundation for a well-adjusted family environment. Take the analogy of global climate impacting the world environment and bring it home to your family and house. Are you building up a caring family environment for posterity? Or will your kids recall memories of dysfunctional relationships that petrify over their recollections of the good times?

Your family's peace of mind is everyone's security blanket. How so? When kids are lovingly nurtured, they quietly spread their influence to their peers at school.

Your kids will be able to stand up for themselves, socialise responsibly, and avoid negative peer pressure encouraging them to act out—or worse—to try drugs, alcohol, and unprotected sex.

That is how subtle influences can be in spreading unseen, but very palpable, energy and vibrations. That is how like attracts like for positive effects according to the Law of Attraction.

You're probably familiar with TV chef Jamie Oliver's lively exhortations to eat well by staying off processed and refined foods. The star of *The Naked Chef* and lately, *Jamie's Ministry of Food* told the *New York Times Magazine,* "Every child should be taught to cook in school, not just talk about nutrition all day. Good food can be made in 15 minutes." Now, that is practical life education 101!

Jamie Oliver's next sentence is even more revealing: "This could be the first generation where the kids teach the parents." With over a billion pounds sterling invested in overhauling school lunches, you bet this is revolutionary. Physical food is important for nourishing strong, healthy bodies.

But even more important, it is revealing that many people are now at the point where we are cognizant of the fact that we are what we eat.

Physical food isn't alone in nourishing body and spirit. More significantly, our total-being wellness also hinges on emotions. The family that loves is also the family that understands the emotional needs of each other; family members extend friendship, are willing to work through issues, and forgive and forget, and allowing bygones to be bygones.

Jamie Oliver, in this same article, also mentioned how he's noticed that certain family members can become jealous of people doing something nice for themselves. This, too, needs to be taken seriously.

It is all part of human nature waiting to be transformed, and it is why personal development is essential in making progress with our lives.

As Mr. Oliver notes, "The key to life is to know what you're good at and stay away from what you're bad at." This is how family members can help each other grow—by showing with gentle love what needs doing and encouraging everyone to blossom and showcase their unique and priceless personality traits.

Here are some ideas to build strong bonds of friendship between your family members. Yes, this means building a sense of trust and camaraderie that good friends commonly share and making it easy for everyone to talk things over instead of turning to the Internet and Google for unrealistic relationship solutions on Web sites:

- ❖ Prepare, cook, and eat dinner together nightly; afterwards, clear away and clean up together as a team.
- ❖ Cultivate an awareness and appreciation for world foods and cultures from your dining room table. Discuss food lore and ethnic dishes and their impacts on world food culture today. Enjoy spicy Indian curries, mouthwatering Italian pizza pies, German bratwurst and beer, Middle Eastern olive oil and falafel, Japanese teriyaki, Chinese fried rice, tasty Nigerian jallof rice with chicken, and Jamaican ackee and salf fish with dumplings.
- ❖ Take turns creating international menus—Hawaiian, Thai, Greek, Mexican, Vietnamese, Ethiopian, and other tasty ethnic cuisines. Discuss how sharing food leads to sharing an appreciation of other cultures and ideas on promoting world peace.
- ❖ Use the dining room table to develop the theme of peaceful feeding. Satisfied and grateful diners make for peaceful global citizens and world travelers!

It's amazing how the food table is such a significant symbol of endearing and enduring sustenance all over the world. Our lives are centred on good food, good vibes, and good company because the appreciative act of sharing through eating impacts and influences our emotions. Good table manners make it easy to diffuse goodwill to and with other cultures and countries.

That is how your family can set forth an impressive "world culture table" when you invite your kids' friends home for dinner. The influence of anything positive (and alas, negative) is bound to spread. Indirectly, you're also quietly offering a public service by showing young people the dynamics of getting along at the dinner table.

Partners & Relationships

> **Know thyself means this, that you get acquainted with what you know, and what you can do.**
>
> **~ Menander**

The main thrust of every successful relationship is how well people get along with themselves and with others. Meaning, it begins with YOU—getting along with you, first. You are a partner unto yourself—where five disparate elements of your being try to get along with each other. Then, after knowing yourself better, it becomes easier to understand what it takes to cultivate and nurture relationships with other people.

How well do you know yourself? Do you love and value you? Have you noticed how sometimes you can actually see a different person responding to situations—as when your heart and inner being looks at how your mind reacts?

That is the 64 million dollar question of questions—who am I? Additionally, what am I supposed to be doing? Why am I not fulfilling my potential when instinctively I feel there are lots more waiting to bubble up from inside of me?

As I pointed out at the very start, **why do we play small?**

We have to begin feeling good about ourselves, in order to grow. It's that positive feeling of like attracting like. Gift yourself your birthright to pull out your potential strengths and powers to fulfil your destiny.

Bottom line? No one can do it for you. You can only make progress when you're confident of whom you are, and where you'd like to go with your personal journey of self-discovery. And, please, always remember to offer to the Universe grateful prayers for all the blessings it's bestowing on you!

> **We make a living by what we get; we make a life by what we give.**
>
> **~ Winston Churchill**

So, how do you start? After knowing yourself first, it's much easier to relate to other people.

For example, if you're looking to attract a compatible partner into your life, it helps to know what your strengths and limitations are.

Are you an impatient person who turns other people off by your impatience? If it were 'yes,' what steps would you need to take to become more patient with yourself and others? How would you make "you" more amenable to other people's suggestions and in working with them?

Or, are you so laid back you don't put forth the energy that is required to cultivate a strong and lasting relationship with a significant other, and all the while hoping the other person makes the requisite overtures first?

Have you asked yourself at the start of any relationship—is this worth putting so much of my time and efforts into, and for the other person, as well? What are my honest assessments of how spending time together will work out? How will I know when to pull out before I'm drained by giving so much emotionally (yes, monetarily as well) that I can't force myself to pull out of the relationship as it's already too late?

And, Oh Boy! Have you heard of couples who can't stop their wedding plans because they would cause too many disruptions and hurt *other* family members—only to divorce a few years later?

Like attracts like in relationships, too. How you put forth energy to attract a life partner depends on the subtle energies you emit. Are your outer words and behaviour contradicting your inner aspirations?

As you're attracting a compatible prospect into your love life, ask how you can value and grow with this person so you both maintain an ongoing healthy relationship.

What does it take for you yourself, and for both of you, to develop a loving partnership that is smooth, sweet, tender, forgiving and to cherish what is lifelong and true to each other?

Occasionally remind yourself that since we vibrate forth unspoken emotions, your positive approval of your loved one does make it easier for you both to get along. As the saying goes, "bite your tongue" when critical thoughts arise, and focus on their strengths instead. Mutual admiration greases the wheel of life smoothly.

Obviously, it begins with knowing yourself, first. Here are three Ground Rules to know and to apply for Personal Development that inevitably pave the way to nurture relationships with your spouse or significant other.

Ground Rule #1. Know that your being is made up of five disparate elements, either working together in making you feel good, or not synchronising well together in making you feel uninspired. They are your:

1 Body. Your dynamic body can either be very willing and inspired to go the extra mile—or flop down like a couch potato. Yes, every element is double-edged.

2 Mind. Your mental faculty that dictates all thoughts and actions, and never gives you a chance for you to follow your heart. Or, your mind can be crystal clear when working with the light of your soul.

3 Vital. Your vital energy fuels your body's get-up-and-go with a dynamic power; your vital can also be aggressive if vital energy is not transformed and purified by taking exercise—that is the reason you feel so good after a workout.

4 Heart. This is the home of all your heartfelt warmth and loving goodness. Except, the heart's double-edged sword can strike fearful and insecure blows to your aspirations in making progress with your life, too.

5 Soul. Your soul is that portion of Divinity, that spark of Eternity at the very core of your existence, lifetime after lifetime. This is the only part of your being that is not double-edged. Your Soul is Eternal. As the *Bhagavad Gita* expounds, no fire, flood nor storm can cleave your Soul.

Ground Rule #2. Now that you know you're not always in harmony with your self because of unsynchronised pulls exerted by varying forces from these five elements of your core being, you'll need to take steps to smoothen out the rough edges. In other words, to align the disparate parts of your being from within—not from without, as we've been taught into thinking and socialised into doing.

That is how we've been *thinking*, not feeling. Get the difference? Our minds have been so much in control of our actions in dictating what it likes to do or not, it's hardly given room for our deeper instincts to surface from the heart-room, let alone for the light of the soul to shine forth!

That is why you've been playing small. Just imagine. If you were to employ all five elements of your being into a coherent whole in synch with the light of your soul, think about how much more you can achieve and amplify the progress you can make with your life!

Ground Rule #3. Let's now see how we can realign ourselves to befriend our Inner Self from the depths of our Being. You can start by doing short daily meditations, prayers, affirmations and visualisations as I've outlined earlier on. The whole idea is *to get going!*

We can do whatever we wish to do provided our wish is strong enough. What do you most want to do? That is what I have to keep asking myself, in the face of difficulties.”

~ Katherine Mansfield

Make a plan. Write down your goals and state your timelines—five minutes of morning meditation; five more at noon before lunch; five more minutes before turning in. Before you know it, you’ll be spending more time meditating because it feels so good. For help on setting and writing your goals visit www.felicityokolo.com on products page for goal setting audio CD.

Meditation is acquiring the art of listening—of listening to inner guidance and protection beaming at your outer being from The Source that is inside everyone.

Keep a journal and make a record of all your personal development activities. It helps to be able to compare notes from day to day. You might be able to discern trends that impact or impede your progress. In the event you need inspiration to keep going, your journal entries will help by re-inspiring you with the progress you’ve made.

Don’t give in to excuses. *You are your own boss*. Don’t let external demands from family and work rob you of developing your true potential. No one can do it for you—only you can commit and expedite your own personal progress!

Let’s now apply the Law of Attraction to how you relate to yourself and to others.

❖ Love yourself as you would others. That is the basic, most elemental act of this law. Love is positive. Loving and honouring your higher self and inviting it to illumine and transform your lower and less positive qualities such as negative thoughts, a critical mind and unwillingness, is taking a very significant first step. Get used to it and apply it daily to affirm your self-worth with Love.

❖ The Law of Attraction states that when you emit feelings of self-worth and positive energy into your environment, you call up these qualities to light up your life. Conversely, if you call up doubt, fear and insecurity, they’ll strangle you, too. The choice is obvious. However, owing to decades of critical control by the mind, we’ve allowed the mind to dictate less than ideal conditions in blocking out positive progress with our hearts and the soul's light. That is why it's imperative to be happy, cheerful and willing to going with divine flow. Life happens. We need to **fly with Life!** Not spiral downwards with fear, insecurity and doubt.

- As I've been pointing out all along, when we play big and allow our light to shine through, we can get along with others famously and inspire them as well on their own journeys of self-discovery. That is what leaders do—inspire others to bring forth their highest and best qualities, so their team advances even more powerfully. Whether at home, at work or with the community at large, positive energy accomplishes more than negativity.
- YOU have the power to therefore illumine and transform negative thoughts into positive outcomes in every relationship. If you've not been getting along with a parent, send love and respect to them, as you would honour thyself. If a co-worker bothers you at work, stop heaping annoying barbs back at them. Once you cut off your critical mind's unrelenting criticisms, your heart will be able to shine forth appreciation and gratitude for how this person contributes to the overall efficacy and functioning of your team.
- While admitting that everyone, including you, is not perfect, always focus on the positive aspects. Remember, like attracts like. Aim to always see the best in everyone and in every situation.
- Don't let physical attributes such as height pull you down. If tall people were smarter, we'd have a whole lot more smarts to work with in the world. If you're a minority ethnic person living in a majority mainstream community, go with the flow and learn to integrate graciously and confidently. My point is—look beyond the physical makeup to uncover your true self.
- Free yourself of the load of a dead albatross hanging around your neck. Don't ever think it's your job to make others happy because a leopard can't change its spots. You are the Number One responsibility for yourself. Besides, you'll inspire others when they see *you* changing into a positive and cheerful person that is also making successful strides with your wealth, health and overall happiness in life!

- ❖ Plus, don't expect a loved one to be what they are not. How many times have you heard of marriages failing because one spouse had set out trying to change the other? Change yourself first, for the better.
- ❖ Have you tried being the first to say 'hello' or to smile? Try it—and feel the amazing love and gratitude emanating from the other person. Let go of the feeling of not being worthy in saying 'hi' and extending a hand of friendship.
- ❖ Love yourself for the clever and notable solutions you've come up with in getting ahead with your family, at work and wherever your golden touch works a magic wand. Celebrate your successes—you've earned them from dint of hard work, ingenuity and the sheer determination of your heroic efforts!
- ❖ Most of all, remember to acknowledge your Creator! Offer back Love and Gratitude with your soulful meditation and earnest prayers. It's this very act of loving unconditionally from the Source of Infinite Love that is enabling us to live a life of divine possibilities. When we offer love and gratitude daily back to the Source, we become even more receptive to divine gifts of grace.

Admittedly, and notwithstanding your best intentions, sometimes Life isn't all smooth sailing. It could be the loss of a loved one, a scary medical diagnosis, the loss of a job, having to adjust to living in a new neighbourhood in a different cultural vein or a marriage gone bust. What to do then?

In her own worst seasons, writer Barbara Kingsolver shares in her book, *High Tide in Tucson: Essays from Now or Never*, that she forced herself, "to look hard, for a long time, at a single glorious thing: a flame of red geranium outside my bedroom window. And then another: my daughter in a yellow dress. And another: the perfect outline of a full, dark sphere behind the crescent moon until I learned to be in love with my life again. Like a stroke victim retraining new parts of the brain to grasp lost skills, I have taught myself joy, over and over again."

Inevitably, we have to face the loss of a loved one—whether through physical death or emotional separation when relationships get severed.

Grief is a traumatic experience. Family and friends show their loving support. They try to make you feel better. And you will feel better after a while—but only after you've reached in deep enough to pull out your inner wealth and strength of making peace with your loss, of appreciating the Gift of Life, by embracing the will to carry on and by prevailing on fond memories for very palpable and tangible reminders of good times—so that you see the light in strengthening your resolve to overcome a personal trauma.

You have to fall in love with your self and your life. You'll be amazed at what your soul's light can gift you—whether the going is good or not so good. Always turn inwards first for answers. Your Best Friend, your Soul, has all the answers.

Hope springs eternal. Why? Because hope invites newness and new beginnings and the courage to move on to greener pastures. This saying is never ever clichéd.

Your inner strength will empower you to meet challenge after challenge along Life's Highway. Welcome Life for enriching you with varied experiences. Offer your heart's Gratitude in living and enjoying Life to the fullest!

Where I was born and where and how I have lived is unimportant. It is what I have done with where I have been that should be of interest.

~ Georgia O'Keeffe, Painter

Inevitably, cutting edge chef Jamie Oliver sums it up succinctly, "It's the battle of life, isn't it, in trying to get the right balance?" He's also right on in saying, "Look, the brilliant and beautiful thing in life is that anyone can do anything!"

So, sharpen your edge, be inspired by other people and what they do. Instead of wallowing in self-pity or being jealous of others, learn from them—and learn from knowing and understanding who you are, and of what YOU are capable of transforming!

Health—Mind-Body Connections

Everyone wants to stay as healthy as possible even in their golden years while enjoying a reasonable quality of life. And, science and new medical technology have made this possible for many.

Yet, not everyone reaches their golden-year milestones, and still remain hale and hearty. The good news—anyone can achieve this goal if they respect the strong mind-body connection that results in a healthy body and dynamic fitness—regardless of chronological age.

How? It's attracting positive energy to continuously renew and re-energise body cells in harmony with the rhythm of the universe.

As I've been showing in my discussions, the Law of Attraction is a powerful magnet of energy vibrations that everyone resonates to, and along with. Quantum physicists refer to this phenomenon as vibrating frequencies that connect random molecules of physical matter and thoughts.

Therefore, the powerful magnet that you are, you attract either positive or negative energy with your thoughts. That is how amazingly forceful the mind-body connection is, whether your thoughts are conscious or not. Your mental energy influences your body's energy.

The mind-body connection is not new. In 1875, William B. Carpenter formalised "Psychoneuromuscular Theory" in his book, *Principles of Mental Physiology*. Over 100 years later, this mind-muscle theory is a soundly proven sports training method used by winning coaches and their super-star athletes.

Today, sports psychologists use variations of PST (Psychological Skills Training) to train athletes to use mental imagery to achieve winning results. It's a technique that Tiger Woods uses to visualise winning golf shots. World tennis champion Andre Agassi is another successful proponent of the mental imagery strategy. Wimbledon tennis champs, American sisters Serena and Venus Williams also actualise winning matches with their mental-muscle or mind-body techniques. Flex your brains and your brawn! You'll never know what you'll miss if you don't try!

Indeed, why should the average Joe or Jane miss out on leveraging their right to mind-body optimum health? *You can* become your own super-star of good health, money and positive relationships. Start now!

If you think only adults benefit from mental imagery, think again. Here's what a study found.

Seven to 10-year old kids were formed into three table tennis teams. Results showed the team of children that had been coached in mental imagery before the game showed more accurate and quality hits compared to the control group of players who were not coached.

Not surprisingly, researchers who authored this study recommended that kids be taught mental imagery at an early age. This way, they could benefit from learning to cultivate better control over their lives starting at an early age.

Psychoneuromuscular or neuropsychology and PST sports training validate the power of the mind in leveraging healthy conditions for the body. Given that a person's power source is located within, the source of all physical healing radiates from this inner core. That is not to say medical intervention isn't necessary in the face of trauma and accidents, but even after surgical intervention, the body's own healing force completes the body's restoration.

Chinese medicine and healing refer to this force as *chi*, Ayurveda or the science of Indian medicine calls it *prana* and the Hawaiians call it *mana*. To feel your chi, close your eyes. Slowly bring both palms together. Do you feel a band of energy subtly surrounding your palms? Your healing force emanates from within. You may have heard of touch therapy where a patient's chronic pains subside or even vanish after the person's chi is rebalanced by a healer's touch.

This is the simplest and most profound key to good health. ***You* have the power to imagine positive healing thoughts with mental imagery using visualisation to achieve whole-being wellness.** To help you further with visualization, visit www.felicityokolo.com to download teleseminar recording on Free Resources page of my interview with Jack Canfield Co-creator of Chicken Soup For The Soul Series on Visualisation.

Remember affirmations? Your road to wellness is immeasurably shortened when you couple visualisation with affirmation. Using both techniques together will increase powerful vibrational frequencies to expedite healing. (Or for any project, such as getting a job promotion, when your strong intentions emanate forth these signals to the universe.)

When we think of female scientists, we think of Madame Marie Curie, three-time Pulitzer Prize-winner for chemistry. However, be pleased to meet Dr. Shirley Ann Jackson. An African-American theoretical physicist and university president of Rennselaer Polytechnic Institute in Troy, New York state, Dr. Jackson is a modern day stellar scientist who is just as impressive in her own imitable ways.

Her powerful persuasive insights are in the September 2009 issue of *O, The Oprah Magazine*. Dr. Shirley Ann Jackson advises, "Follow your passion with persistence, magnified by intense preparation. Use compassion and courage to weave a strong web of connections. Use focused excellence to drive achievements and gain wisdom. It is through the combination of all these things that your power will reveal itself to you."

So, there you have it. The secret to power in every facet of your life is to effectively and persistently harness your mind, vital and heart.

Additionally, Dr. Jackson reminds us: "You must be prepared; you must commit the time, energy and effort required to achieve. Be persistent. All of this requires courage: the courage of your convictions, the courage to get started, and the courage to keep going. The magnitude and reach of your power is up to you."

In other words, the sky is just the beginning. Don't hold back. Don't think and play small. It also bears repeating that all areas of our being are inter-related—body, mind, vital, heart and soul. Influences, vibrations and impacts are felt systemically in a person's entire being. No part of your being can be singled out as being more resourceful or powerful; synchronicity is the name of the game. As the ripple effect analogy shows, hitting the water with just one stone has the power to ripple waves across the pond.

Make your own waves to heal and to prosper, and in relating to yourself, others and the environment where you live and work.

No pain of challenge, no gain indeed. Plain and simple. Allow yourself to soak up the principles of neuropsychology with some easy affirmations such as these below.

It's pointless repeating mantras without passion or intensity. A mantra is a sacred invocation from the very depths of your being. Your sincere intensity will be relayed to, and picked up by, the universe. Honour this exercise by saying your mantras (or affirmations) in a quiet place. Remember to offer gratitude after you're done for the opportunity to relay your wishes for positive and healthy outcomes that will impact you, family members, the environment and workplace conditions.

- ❖ Say: "I am Whole, Perfect, Strong, Powerful, Loving, Harmonious and Happy." I love this quote from Charles Haanel!
- ❖ <u>Say: When I forgive, I heal and recover with extra strength.</u> Strength to pursue positive projects instead of holding on to grudges that devour precious energy.
- ❖ <u>Say: I have the power to heal from within.</u> This power is immense and immeasurable because it's from my Soul, The Supreme Source of all Being.
- ❖ <u>Say: I love myself as a healthy, wholesome person, from the soles of my feet to the hair on my head.</u> Appreciate the

beautiful physical attributes they gift your personality and appearance. Have you taken time for a pedicure to treat your toes, soles of your feet and ankles? An appointment at the hair stylist to trim those uneven wispy strands? Affirm the integrity and beauty of your physical body that has served you so dutifully all these years.

- ❖ Say: I'm letting go of my critical mind. Transform your mind with the light of your soul. Allow your heart-power to illumine your critical and faultfinding mental faculties with love, compassion, forgiveness, peace, joy, faith, respect and trust.
- ❖ Say: There is no such thing as an incurable disease. Norman Cousins, who was diagnosed with "an incurable disease," laughed himself to wellness by watching funny movies for three straight months. Laughter is a positive frequency; that is why it heals physically, mentally and emotionally.
- ❖ Say: I'm eternally grateful to the Universe for my good health. You can substitute "Universe" with The Buddha or Christ, a favourite saint, Our Lady, Mother Earth or any tangible manifestation of a higher power that is meaningful to you. Offering gratitude is never ever out of style.
- ❖ Say: My happiness wealth is my body's health. As I've been saying all along, happiness is a positive force. When you're happy, you're in control of your own well-being. San Francisco cardiologist, Dr. Dean Ornish wrote in his book *Love and Survival* that love is the real power to heal. Love, happiness and forgiveness are all free. What do you have to lose, except by not visualising and affirming them to your benefit? (Although the trick is—you have to unlearn old ways of thinking to start thinking in new ways, and that means putting in the effort to getting started.)
- ❖ Say: Inner and outer food blesses me with an integrated and wholesome being. That is why physical health and emotional well-being are interconnected, and the harmonious flow of mind-body or mental-muscle power is vital in promoting good health.

Good health is the true wealth. Without good health, you'll not be able to work nor take care of yourself and your family. The power of your immune system is only as strong as the power of your positive thinking. Just for fun, think good thoughts and hold out an arm. Ask someone to press it down; they'll have a hard time doing it. Next, switch your thoughts to negative vibes of suspicion, doubt and fear. When this person presses on your outstretched arm, it'll drop easily. Honour your mind-body connection for optimum health!

Physical Strength—Transforming Dynamic Energy

Physical strength is vital energy that enables us to move around. Have you stopped and wondered how it would be like if you couldn't get out of bed one morning? Or, perhaps you have on a bleak morning, for whatever reason, before tumbling out of bed.

That is why physical energy is often referred to as "vital energy" that is fundamental for your body to use. You owe it to yourself to renew and revitalise your physical energy. When people don't, they end up suffering chronic fatigue, also known as adrenal fatigue. That is when it's really impossible for the person to get out of bed.

To prevent this unkind misfortune to ever happen to your body, learn to listen to your inner voice, your intuition or instincts. If you're tired out and need a nap, go ahead and do it. It's amazing how 15 minutes of zzzz'sss can revitalise your whole being. Upon waking, you carry on more mentally alert, with more vital energy and a positive attitude that is life-altering!

Just trust yourself, then you will know how to live.

~ Johann Wolfgang von Goethe

Like all things finite, your vital energy needs renewing which can come from a variety of ways in accessing the source. Such as:

- Rest and down time in between projects and activities
- Sleep as a natural response to your circadian rhythm with daily normal needs for an adult at 7-8 hours
- A power nap does wonders to renew the total being, leaving you refreshed to tackle any assignment with vigour
- Exercise to transform restless and stressful energy into dynamic new energy. That is why your mind and body feel so good after a physical workout

- ❖ Meditate to calm and soothe your senses, release negative and pent-up frustrations and to re-energise you
- ❖ Affirmations to confirm positive energy renewal
- ❖ Visualisations to mentally evoke and envision desired physical and material outcomes
- ❖ Time out for fun hobbies that promote positive energy such as gardening, baking bread or volunteering at your children's school once a week or at the library
- ❖ Journal your thoughts and aspirations as you write your heart out. That is you, writing your own book! Keeping a journal is a healing therapy that is both personal and cathartic. You write as much as you like and as often as you're inclined. There's no deadline to meet. It's a unique exercise where you allow your stream of consciousness to express itself. And, when you need inspiration, your journal entries never fail to gift you with a lift as needed
- ❖ Prayer is the time-honoured homage to our Source that everyone intuitively turns to. Make time every day for soulful prayers to guide and protect your actions. It's also therapeutic when we confess our limitations and missteps. That is why some churches emphasise the confessional approach
- ❖ Vacations are well worth the R and R (rest and recreation) expense, to return to work with a positive mindset
- ❖ Call up a friend. Non-gossip exchanges refresh and inspire when good friends talk heart-to-heart. The Mayo Clinic, a top U.S. health care and medical research centre, has studied how family and friends are vital for patients to recover and heal again

With today's running around in trying to getting ahead, it may appear counter-productive in making time to get to know your deeper self, and to renew yourself when needed.

For example, it's time taken out from your regular schedule to meditate, for a short ten-minute nap or to write journal entries.

However, what's less productive is to make yourself a master multi-tasker in attempting to tackle as many projects as you can, all at once. Multi-tasking is a myth. It's not time management that we need.

Rather, you need self-management - a better management of your scarce and limited energy resources—by attracting positive energy to enrich you in as many ways as you need and like!

Once you know and understand yourself better, you'll become more expert in managing your energy reserves to maximise living Life to your fullest potential. You have the key to unlock the stronghold to your inner treasures to bring them out. Getting started is the key.

TO DO: TRANSFORMATIVE ENERGY RITUALS

Restless energy is a by-product of spent energy that is just waiting and itching to renew itself. Here are some creative ways to transform energy productively:

- Unlike circadian rhythms, which occur once every 24 hours, our **ultradian rhythms** are programmed to only focus on one thing at a time, and for only 90-120 minutes each time. One of world's most influential productivity experts is W. Edwards Deming who invented the concept of "chunking." Chunking means planning and organising your activities together in small blocks of uninterrupted chunks of time. You'll find you get more done, and it'll do wonders to reduce your stress levels instead of, "OMG, having to finish a BIG project." You could set a timer to buzz you about every 90-120 minutes at work, to shift project gears accordingly.
- Researchers at Harvard and Columbia universities studied women who were involved in short bursts of aerobic activity. Each aerobic burst was less than 60 seconds. But, because these women were able to completely rest and recover, just doing 60 aerobic bursts a month (or 2 aerobic bursts a day) actually strengthened their immune systems and enhanced cardiovascular health. Aerobic activity purifies lethargic energy; be sure to factor in rest and recovery time, though.
- Bedtime ritual. Go to bed at the same time every night and wake up at the same time, too. This helps your body recover physically and emotionally to power through the next day's activities. Have at least 7-8 hours of sleep. The National Sleep Foundation (an American non-profit) recommends keeping your bedroom thermostat between 54-75 degrees Fahrenheit (15-25 degree centigrade) at night (it'll also save on your energy bill).

> ❖ When you wake up refreshed and energised, you're powered up to perform the best you can—physically, mentally, intellectually and with a positive mindset and energy levels that peps up other people, too.

This is the "simple secret" of personal development. By enlarging your capacity to build on your physical, mental, vital and spiritual energies, you rally forth more capabilities to live a positive and energetic life. It doesn't stop there. Other people lucky enough to work with you will feel your ripple effect—and will want to know what empowers you. That is inspiring them on, too!

Personal growth is powerful, life-changing and free to acquire—and available to everyone!

You only have to want to do it by setting aside a few minutes daily with any of the exercises I've described thus far. Go with two or three that instinctively call to you; they're the ones that motivate you more easily in getting started. There on out, the positive reinforcements that you begin to enjoy will motivate you to keep going

Plus, you can always contact me for more coaching sessions by emailing felicity@felicityokolo.com.

Life Areas Recap

I've outlined seven important areas in your life that are all interdependent on each other. Without nurturing these areas, personal development cannot progress as quickly and effectively.

Life happens. Challenging life situations occur—when a relationship breaks up, a business venture goes under, a home is foreclosed, a medical emergency brings on unexpected traumatic emotions or losing a loved one.

When unfortunate events happen, we're better equipped to face them—if we understand what to do. Knowing our inner strengths enables us to understand what it takes to transform the unillumined outer parts of the being with positive energies. We *can* start playing big and bigger on our life stage.

The opposite happens, as well. When we're less informed about ourselves, but are thrust onto the public and world stage with sudden fame and celebrity recognition, we're less able to handle the spotlight that Life is suddenly shining on us. We've read of top models and performers turning to drugs to deal with the pressures of going professional because they didn't know how to cope with growing pains.

My sincere hope is for you to discover the different parts of your being in time—in order to live Life as joyfully, healthily and prosperously as possible. Follow your bliss! Follow your heart to realise your potential! Follow your dreams waiting to transform your life!

I've listed and explained many techniques for personal development. Keep playing with them; listen to your intuition to tweak them as needed to make them work for you.

After all, YOU are the master of your own destiny. As the Chinese philosopher Lao Tzu exhorts, "*Mastering others is strength, mastering yourself is true power.*"

I know that knowing and understanding yourself is the foundation to success in every area of your life. The analogy I use is this: "Imagine your life as a building. If this building does not have a good solid foundation, anytime a little wind blows, it'll fall down, or you'll have to keep repairing and fixing it."

So, too, in your life, if you don't know and understand yourself, every time little things or misfortunes blow into your life, you'll crumble and find yourself constantly trying to repair and fix your outer life—instead of spending time that could be used on other more constructive projects.

Sometimes though, you won't be able to repair or fix your house properly. But if you know and understand yourself before calamity strikes, you'll be better equipped to handle life's challenges with minimal fixing or repairing.

That is how the power of personal development can aid, rescue and empower you on to infinite wealth, good health, love and happiness.

Chapter 2.

SIX HUMAN NEEDS

> ***Life is a promise; fulfil it.***
>
> ***~ Mother Teresa***

There are six human needs I'm going to explain and explore in this chapter. These needs drive our universal desires to have love, health and wealth to nurture us as satisfied and fulfilled beings:

- Certainty
- Growth
- Significance
- Love and connection
- Variety
- Contribution

1) Certainty

As surely as the law of gravity anchors us to the ground, we also need to be true to ourselves. That is what self-awareness is all about—in contributing to personal growth by acknowledging your self-worth. It means knowing with **CERTAINTY** who you are with your values and beliefs, and where you're headed to with your life.

We also need to apply certainty in living a secure life. Certainty about where our finances are coming from so we're not perpetually worried and anxious.

It's human nature to need certainty in very basic areas of our lives—such as paying rent and bills on time. These are basic needs that have to be addressed. It is how we meet and deal with these needs that show how well we know and understand ourselves.

Of course, too much certainty can also lead to boredom. We need to strike a balance, as for everything else in life.

Self-awareness identifies your true worth—for example, self-respect, integrity, honesty, simplicity and sincerity; including insecurity, unwillingness, unfriendliness, intolerance and denial. Please continue identifying attributes that you feel describe YOU below:

- ❖ ____
- ❖ ____
- ❖ ____
- ❖ ____
- ❖ ____
- ❖ ____

Do not be judgmental as you do this exercise. It's a bit like journaling where you articulate your aspirations, hopes and wishes. List your fears and doubts too, to expel them from your consciousness—there, done!

Next, list the positives and then the negatives. After listing them, see if you can rearrange them by opposite pulls; for example, lining up "diligent" next to "procrastinate." Keep on maintaining neutrality by not judging your traits as you list them.

After you're done, do you see patterns or trends? Do your lists show a more, or less, optimistic person at work?

If pessimistic traits overpower your positives, do not despair! This is the whole point of doing this personal development exercise—to discover personal limitations so you can begin to work on leveraging your positive strengths to transform and illumine your perceived limitations.

It's no "sin" to uncover mistakes within us. What's sinful is to be so mired in ignorance that we don't allow our higher attributes to shine forth to illumine misery and overcome smallness. When you do this, you're giving yourself and others permission to be liberated, so you can uncover light and potential from within. (If you'll recall, this reiterates Marianne Williamson's strong call to action that I'd quoted earlier).

Celebrate your strengths and weaknesses! It's actually strength on your part: 1) to look at your less positive traits, 2) acknowledge you need to change them for the better, and 3) embark on self-transformation to transcend, for newer heights of self-satisfaction.

Welcome change with open arms, not trepidation! This leads us to the next section—growing BIG with your talents.

2) Growth

Do you seek a better job? Do you pray for better conditions at work with co-workers and your surroundings? Do you wish to see your children succeed at school, excel in sports and win scholarships?

These inclinations and deep-seated longings are human needs in wanting to get ahead with our lives and for our loved ones.

It's called—**GROWTH and it is one of the highest human needs.** It's humanity's constant striving to get a better education in order to sustain an above-average livelihood, to raise a loving and successful family and to keep growing emotionally and economically, and being employed with prospects for promotion.

Personal growth takes a back seat the moment you find you're less than motivated in getting ahead. This happens all too often, especially when we're faced with loss—of a parent, sibling or good friend; retrenchment; or a scary medical diagnosis.

Yet, these are the very moments in our lives when we need to dig out from under—and keep growing even stronger. When we dig deeper, and our inner cries for help are sincere and fervent, we usually find the light of the soul guiding us on to tangible solutions.

That is how Oprah learned to dig out from under the abuses she suffered as a child. Reading opened up new worlds of imagination and thrilling adventures for her. Fired by her dreams and determination to do better and to live a life filled with inspiration and aspiration, Oprah became driven to grow. So can you, or anyone, for the record!

Now, please ask yourself these questions and jot down your answers:

A) How happy am I with my life, generally?

____

____

____

B) How happy am I at work?

____

____

____

C) If I passed on tomorrow, what are my biggest regrets?

____

____

____

D) If I passed on tomorrow, what are my biggest achievements?

____

____

____

E) If I could break out of my present situation, what would I like to do?

____

____

____

F) If I could do something *now* with my life, what would I do right away?

____

____

____

Hone in on the immediacy of wanting to do something with your life that ***you've always wanted to do***—take photography lessons, switch to a new career, look for a new neighbourhood and house to move to, or spend time meditating to discover your new calling that is going to fulfil you more deeply and outwardly, too.

As the saying goes, no pain, no gain. In order to grow, we must accept growing pains that accompany the growth process.

Pain of failure, pain of an unwarranted financial discovery or pain of taking a wrong turn that led to an auto accident are all part of incidents on Life's highway.

Learning from Life's missteps is key to recovery and success.

That is why the law of attraction makes so much sense in simplifying your life as it increases the chances of attracting positive experiences. Not that anyone can ever escape misfortunes, but *you can be in control* of taking steps to lessen their impact.

When you consciously want to grow positive experiences with your life, your magnetic longings will attract and deliver to you a preponderance of positive growth over negative experiences.

It's not about whether liking or disliking personal growth – it's about whether someone wants to grow and develop, or not. Admittedly, it's hard to unlearn bad habits. However, you have to admit, too, that once you begin to experience the benefits of positive growth, you'll want to keep on uncovering more nuggets from within to grace your outer life. Keep moving! Keep paddling—upstream or downstream, it doesn't matter—keep unlearning to learn the new! Keep on learning, in order to keep growing!

The result? You're happier, more socially adept at going with the flow and starting to enjoy the benefits of optimal living conditions.

SIMPLE POCKET MEDITATION

One of the most practical life exercises is to grow a positive appreciation for safe driving—for you and for others, for example (it can also be applied to other situations). An ounce of prevention is worth pounds of cure later. Here's what to do:

1 Before driving off, as your car warms up, meditate for one minute on safety. You're signalling to the universe a positive sign—for your safety, other drivers and pedestrians. Focus on a medal of St. Christopher (patron saint of safe driving), the Christ, your spiritual master, or simply close your eyes and tune inwards.

2 Upon arrival, offer another minute, of Gratitude meditation.

3 That is all it takes. Two minutes of intense energy sharing that impacts the safety of many others. As we grow to appreciate ourselves, we also appreciate others in a similar light. That is the beauty of GROWTH—personal and inter-personal.

4 Plus, taking 5 trips in one day, gifts you 10 minutes of meditation.

5 **You can also adapt this pocket meditation to any situation. Even if outcomes are not as expected, you'll still be calm and poised. Meditation is a practical life tool to enhance every endeavour.**

3) Significance

The **SIGNIFICANCE** and benefits of your self-discoveries are yours to admire and to appreciate. You've put in the efforts to cultivate positive growth.

Now, take time to reflect on the progress you've made. Again, do not be judgmental about the amount, or lack, of perceived gains. The journey is what matters—the effort you've expended on your quest.

The results of your personal quest are positively reassuring in placing the significance of who you are as a loving and respected person.

We all strive to differentiate ourselves from others. We like to distinguish ourselves at work and at play. We all want to feel significant and important in life, but too much trying to be different could lead to feeling unconnected and distant from people leading to a need for love & connection, which is the opposite of significance.

It is how we meet and deal with this need that shows how well we know and understand ourselves.

TO DO: PERSONAL GROWTH RESUME

It's handy to have benchmark comparisons of how you started, and what you've achieved, along your journey of self-discovery.

I suggest starting a "3R Resume" to—Review, Re-write and Re-evaluate your life's goals every 3-4 months.

For example, a workplace resume for self-evaluation might include probing some of these areas:

PERSONAL OBJECTIVE: To Achieve Job Satisfaction

HONOURS/AWARDS: Employee of the Month, May 2005

EXPERIENCE: I.T Trouble-Shooter

STRENGTHS: Enthusiastic about new job, creative problem-solver

SKILLS & INTERESTS: MAC and PC platforms; cyber security

MY OBSERVATIONS TODAY (10 Oct. 2009): *Answer honestly your personal assessment of: how you've been doing; why is your job not giving you as much joy 4.5 years later; what can you do to perk up your enthusiasm; can you tie visible goals to accomplish that your supervisor can also see and appreciate?*

GOALS TO ACHIEVE IN 3 MONTHS: Positive HR feedback; a raise or more employee perks such as free parking or a paid commuter pass.

~~~

Additionally, you can apply personal growth goals to other areas such as increasing financial resources, meeting a life partner and simply being happier and more fulfilled with your life.

Your journal entries or notes will reveal steps to take in making and achieving your significance felt by you and by others. Reflect on them. Meditate on them. Pray for your soul's guidance to show you the way.
~~~

As you'll notice, you're also deepening your spiritual growth by growing personally. That is the beauty of personal growth—the inner sallies forth to embrace and guide the outer.

That is quite a breakthrough from previous mental and vital actions taking precedence over your heartfelt intuition yearning to connect with you, isn't it?

Other people can feel and see the "new you." Obviously, you'll look different. Your attitudes are more encouraging to your self and others. Your conduct will reveal a new surefootedness, by being more confident.

Before you know it, your magnetic personality starts igniting similar quests for personal growth in your friends, family and co-workers, too.

Another striking sign of making progress is how recurring situations surface as you refine your self-awareness for personal growth. For example, you might notice how similar work situations are with various managers. It could be a lack of management skills such as their inability to delegate without micromanaging—while the rest of the team is more concerned about working smoothly together for productive outcomes.

Whatever each new situation brings forth, you're now more equipped and prepared to meet them headlong—by 1) accepting them, 2) working through them personally and immediately with family or team members, and 3) concerned about doing and giving your best at all times, while being unattached to results.

That is the significance of personal growth—in deepening self-awareness, with others and your environment.

Let's now do this exercise. Without evaluating how much you've learned or not learned, simply please list seven significant changes you've seen in yourself and are now facing:

❖ ______________________________

❖ ______________________________

❖ ______________________________

❖ ______________________________

❖ ______________________________

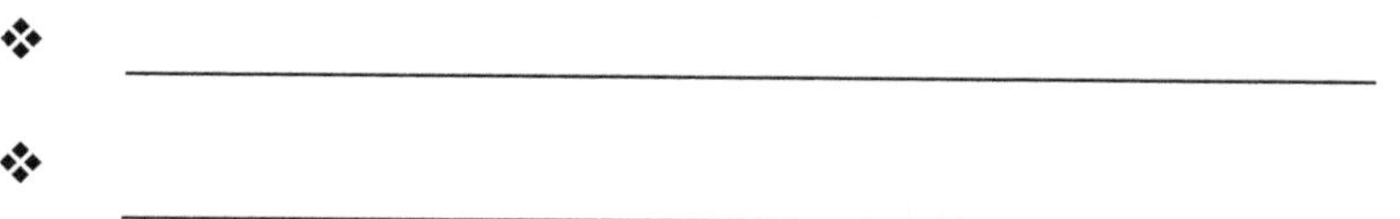

What do you see are dominant forces awakening in you? What do you think your Soul's Light is trying to show you? Journal your discoveries; refer to them for ongoing revelations that inform.

I'm going to relate the power of your CERTAINTY, GROWTH and SIGNIFICANCE of the new changes you'll experience by sharing the story of one amazing person.

Donna Brazile broke the glass ceiling when she became the first African-American to manage a major presidential campaign for U.S. Vice-President Al Gore in 2000. Why and how did she do it?

First, Donna Brazile was certain about her goals: *"I came into this world anxious to be a part of it. I wanted to find my place at the table. I wanted to be successful. I want to make a difference in presidential politics. I want to educate and inform. I want to connect to the next generation. One day I want us to put a woman in the White House."*

Second, although Donna Brazile knew she could accomplish her professional goals by working hard, she did not lose sight of her personal goals. Her sentiments include: *"I want to practice nonviolence. I want to practice joy. I want to learn from my enemies, even if all I learn is not to be like them."*

Her ultimate goal in life? *"I want to get the last word. I want to do a little bit of everything, and when I'm not stirring some pot somewhere or creating some drama, then I want to be alone in my garden."*

As a respected commentator on American television networks, from PBS-TV to CNN-TV and ABC News, Donna Brazile knows what she wants to do with her life, from dreaming big.

Her ambitions started when she was nine. Donna Brazile went door-to-door campaigning for a political candidate. Her desire in doing it at the time? This person had promised the kids a playground in her New Orleans neighbourhood.

Never underestimate the power of your determination and volition in dreaming BIG, and the results that will follow and inspire you throughout your life!

4) Love & Connection

LOVE makes the world go around. Or, love makes life revolve and evolve more smoothly when you use your heart to communicate feelings, however wordlessly they may be expressed through outer actions. How many kinds of love can we count?

Puppy Love comes and goes, with fond memories as gifts of remembrance.

Conditional Love can hardly be called "true love" when expectations run rampant of quid pro quo.

Unrequited Love could possibly be the hardest to endure yet human passions go to uncontrollable excesses to manifest unreturned affection and advances.

Unconditional Love is an offering from the very depths of your heart to loved ones and close friends without expectation of repayment.

There is, however, a common thread through all these different manifestations of love—by reaching out to another person. It's human nature to want to be loved and feel connected to other persons and to belong to groups.

Have you observed your vital or mind offering different kinds of love while reaching out to someone? It wouldn't hurt to catch yourself the next time you offer love to see what kind of love is actually being offered.

These are fascinating insights of self-awareness that reveal how we fulfil such an important basic human need and to see if these actions need to be changed to reflect your innermost, authentic emotions.

On a group level, we express our affection in subtly different ways. For example, during get-togethers for the holidays, family dynamics span at least two to three generations. Love heals when we share in give-and-take. As the saying goes, *"it is better to be on the giving side than on the receiving end."* (Holidays are healing and restorative—if the hostess hasn't whipped herself into a frenzy to be the world's best hostess.)

A person's expression of love also reveals their levels of confidence and social maturity. In 1995, Daniel Goleman, Ph.D., and a former science reporter for the *New York Times* wrote *Emotional Intelligence* (EQ) to show a new way of measuring intelligence instead of the old IQ standard. It included a person's emotional maturity in interacting with others.

Soon EQ was expanded to include social factors, becoming SEL or "Social and Emotional Learning." Schools took off in expanding on the resurgence of mind-emotion connections under the rubric of, "affective neuroscience." This is an important behavioural development in measuring how people relate to each other whether favourably, or not.

Now, SEL is part of many school curricula around the world. SEL skills are taught in character development education, anti-bullying, violence and drug prevention and discipline education.

Research shows that from elementary school on up, students with higher SEL levels are faster learners and can better adapt emotionally to any situation in life. In short, students schooled in social and emotional intelligence progress faster in all areas of personal and scholastic development.

I'm including SEL in this section because it is a valuable skill to acquire for personal development. It's also used by the Harvard School of Business in teaching CEOs, executives and managers how to effectively show appreciation and connect emotionally for positive and productive outcomes.

There's no doubt that a fundamental human need is the ability to show and to get love. Like a flower that inspires with an attractive fragrance, LOVE fills a deep basic need for everyone to be accepted and therefore to feel connected emotionally for positive outcomes.

Of course, too much of anything brings about an imbalance—as when seeking too much love and in wanting to connect with others can lead to co-dependency and a lack of self-esteem.

Love is nurturing energy that everyone responds to naturally—and the more persuaded you are in giving it, the more it returns many times over to gift you in unexpected ways. Love on!

5) Variety

Just as love makes the world go around, human beings also need to feel fulfilled from a **VARIETY** of life experiences. How boring would life be without different foods, different cultural traditions to enjoy, different countries to visit and just as many varied personalities to interact with?

Of course, too much variety can also be overwhelming. Again, striking a balance is necessary.

Variety is indeed the spice of life and opposite of certainty. Have you yearned for life experiences that you've yet to fulfil?

Please list them now:

- ❖ ______________________________
- ❖ ______________________________
- ❖ ______________________________

- ❖ ______________________________
- ❖ ______________________________
- ❖ ______________________________

For each, ask, "What's keeping me from doing it?" Be honest in identifying reasons why you haven't taken the necessary steps to achieve your dreams.

Then, challenge yourself to action. Pick the dream experience that you can realistically apply yourself to whole-heartedly as soon as possible. List action steps to take; then cross off each step after completing it.

By the time you come to the last action step, reward yourself for having been courageous in advancing another positive stride for personal growth—while fulfilling a basic human need to be fulfilled with a VARIETY of diverse experiences.

Now that you've started, don't stop. Keep on working down your dream list until you've crossed off every dream item you've yearned to try.

This is also how you stretch your imagination with realistic accomplishments, and to keep on boosting your self-confidence by overcoming reluctance and the unwillingness to try new things.

6) Contribution

As we keep growing in our journey of self-awareness and awareness of the larger community, we continue to expand our consciousness to include the world at large. We tune in. We watch. We listen. We ponder. We try to provide solutions to perceived problems.

As we've seen, personal growth is not an isolated individual process of development. Our light does shine forth to touch others, and motivate them on to seeking their own bliss and peace, too.

This also sets in motion a greater awareness for social etiquette. How do a person's thoughts, speech and actions impact those around them, while giving back kinder intentions to the universe at large?

It isn't a bad idea actually, to catch oneself working on:

1 Putting forth more positive thoughts and ideas

2 Less profane figures of speech and out with cussing!

3 Sending encouraging words instead of critical messages.

Stretching even more, can you imprint a positive impact on the larger community by volunteering your time, expertise and financial contributions? The inner wealth of unconditional giving and contributing back to community and the environment cannot be overstated, nor be understated. Tune in to community needs.

By giving, you set in motion positive wavelengths that expand, and impact results and outcomes far more than the mind can envision.

That is the Law of Attraction at work in connecting personal aspirations with universal aspirations to lend a helping hand wherever and whenever it's needed. Give with your heart and soul, without any expectation of reward.

The more creative you are, the more impact your contributions become. We see this in the next exemplary story of personal development in an enterprising Japanese woman with her innovative ideas of social responsibility, while growing a profitable business with an environmental CONTRIBUTION.

Yumi Someya lives in Tokyo. As you know, the Japanese love their tempura as much as Americans love their hamburgers. Tempura is deep-fried seafood and vegetables coated in a light rice-flour batter. Every year, close to 200,000 tons of cooking oil is used for frying.

What to do? Yumi Someya persuaded her family's cooking oil recycling business to turn cooking oil into biofuel. *Time* magazine (October 5, 2009) reports that vegetable diesel fuel (VDF) emits no sulphur oxides and half the particulate matter of conventional diesel. It's also very affordable, although vehicles do smell like mobile kitchens.

Yumi Someya tuned into her environment and her family's enterprise—and came up with win-win-win solutions for a remarkable act of social responsibility that went on to produce profitable business opportunities, while being kind to the environment!

Take the time to ask:

- ❖ How should I contribute? What can I do?
- ❖ Do I tune in to my intuition and try to listen to what's needed with my contribution?
- ❖ Who have I hurt, and are they still mad at me; what reasonable recourse can I contribute to make it right again?

- How can I contribute by being more caring?
- What can I contribute to make my home a loving and peaceful sanctuary for my family? How can family members contribute?
- What can I contribute to make my workplace a more harmonious and productive environment?
- What community volunteerism excites me, so it's win-win-win for all sides, you, the community and the environment when we give back?
- How can I optimise my contributions?

The ability to contribute back to others and the environment is truly the other one of our highest human needs. Why? Because human beings are fundamentally altruistic; we like to give and in so doing, receive approbation without having to seek outer approval from anyone.

Approbation is a healing energy that gifts by re-energising our spirits and stamina. Have you noticed how, when you enjoy what you're doing, it makes you more energetic? That is because you're contributing good, positive energy that reflects back to blessing you with even more energy.

The secret to good will is that it comes back to heal and bless us even more—when we give of ourselves totally and unconditionally.

Six Human Needs Recap:

There we have it—the six human needs every person needs to fulfil and maintain. When we work on developing them, we are generating our inert powers into impressive outer manifestations.

What Power we each have inside us! Now that you're starting out on your personal journey of self-discovery, keep growing, stretching and reaching out for infinite possibilities and opportunities to bless you!

With proper nurturing, these lifelong needs will empower and enrich you from within—with natural energies that touch and transform your personal development and impact others, as well.

Chapter 3.

THREE HUMAN DESIRES TO EMBRACE-LOVE, HEALTH & WEALTH

Real power is usually unspectacular, a simple setting aside of fear that allows the free flow of love. But it changes everything.

~ Martha Beck

In the previous chapter, we discussed why love is a strong basic need for inner fulfilment. In this chapter, I'm going to show you how love can spill over as a desire that is as potent a magnet as health and wealth are, to enrich you even more!

1) Love

"Can't buy me love," sang the Beatles in their hit song that is decades old, yet refreshingly spot on with its poignant reminder.

Sure, pseudo-love situations can be bought—good times, expensive gifts of jewellery and trips abroad. But once the material veneer fades, no lasting fragrance of **LOVE** fills the air, let alone the heart.

How come? LOVE is an authentic feeling that can*not* be rehearsed, acted out or played out if the chemistry isn't there, or if it's not felt or sincerely expressed.

Love can become a genuine force for personal change in your life if you start by loving yourself. Learn to forgive yourself for every little booboo. That is why missteps are worth their weight in gold because they are stepping-stones that help you learn to avoid future mistakes.

Reward yourself after finishing projects with watching a video. Pamper your body and senses to a home-spa by luxuriating in a warm lavender bath. Shop for a special gift for a loved one, as giving is as effective as loving when you give of yourself in material ways.

Start making notes of *when* you treated yourself nicely and *how*. Note, too, your emotions towards yourself—did you feel better, became more motivated to tackle cleaning the bathroom and dared yourself to train for a marathon to show that you can take on challenges?

Did you see yourself making life-altering moves that brought more satisfaction and joy to you on deeper levels?

Inevitably, loving yourself also means spreading love and joy to others. That is where inspiration is another magnetic frequency that touches others on a deeper level as well. Be serious about implementing smart actions in loving yourself unconditionally.

Please list at least 10 ways you can start appreciating yourself whole-heartedly. At the same time, visualise how self-appreciation can empower you to positively face challenging situations at work, with neighbours and applying for a new job—and any situation you want to make progress with.

I appreciate myself for:

1. ______________________________

2. ______________________________

3. ______________________________

4. ______________________________

5. ______________________________

6. ______________________________

7. ______________________________

8. ______________________________

9. ______________________________

10. ______________________________

EXERCISE: LOVING INTENTIONS & JOURNALING

1. **How do I appreciate my body for the wealth of good health it's blessing me with?**
2. **How do I appreciate my mind's clear thinking every time it cuts right through indecision?**
3. **How do I appreciate my vital energy in providing me the energy to power through my daily activities?**
4. **How do I appreciate my heart for the courage it shows in defeating fear, self-doubt and insecurity?**
5. **How do I appreciate my Soul for it's boundless encouragement in the face of seemingly insurmountable odds?**

Journal your loving wishes into "your book" and at the forefront of your emotional consciousness. Keep these loving intentions sacred and secret. It's true that sceptical energy (a negative force) from other people can diminish the power of your pure intentions.

Powerful as love is as a desire to nourish and heal you, it's also a powerful energy force to share and nurture others with. When you desire to offer love, people intuitively pick up on it. Love is an innate energy that knows no boundaries. Love transcends every situation.

For instance, while travelling, you may have stopped at a roadside stall to buy fruit. When you sincerely express appreciation for the farmer's lovely produce and hard physical labour that went into producing their fruit, chances are, if your praise is pure, you'll be presented with extra pieces.

It's happened to me often enough in various situations of expressing and sharing love that it reinforces our basic human desire to *want* to give love unconditionally. In so doing, you connect on a deeper level with your magnetic personality that enriches everyone profoundly.

It makes you feel good. When you feel good, it's love at work. Everyone benefits because LOVE brings out the best in us.

2) Health

As I've pointed out before, health is wealth. Without your health, you cannot move your body nor accomplish anything. It's all the more evident when you lose your health. Hence the universal desire for acquiring and maintaining good health.

Let's then use the *desire* to stay healthy as a motivational tool for life-altering enhancements to achieve quality of life. What areas of your life would you like to heal, physically and emotionally?

Please list six areas (three each for physical and emotional) you'd like to bring healing energy to:

1 (For example, better dental hygiene)
____

2
____

3
____

4 (For example, lessen my angry outbursts)
____

5
____

6
____

To set into motion your desire to heal naturally, broadcast your healthful intentions to the universe.

In return, be open to nuances and messages from your intuition, a radio talk show or a casual exchange with a neighbour who ever so coincidentally recommended gargling with salt water to cure a sore throat—just when you needed to hear this!

It's not amazing anymore when you welcome the Law of Attraction into your conscious wavelength and positive intentions. Sending out positive reminders to yourself and others grows exponentially. It's ether social-site networking making the right connections and effecting miracles!

EXERCISE: HEALTHY WEALTHY MOVES

- ❖ Imagine your healthy body just waiting for you to call forth a beautiful form and its metabolic systems to function even more consciously. During an afternoon break, instead of reaching for a Cadbury bar, close your eyes and imagine your dynamic body gifting you resources of stamina you never thought possible before. Gratefully accept these gifts from your body—and resolve to put your newfound dynamic awareness into action whenever you feel yourself wilting.
- ❖ Soulfully invoke your heart's Light to shine a torch into a turbulent mind room that needs illumining. Imagine your mind crystal clear after a soulful meditation. That is when your soul's light is at its best in illumining your thoughts and actions. Don't judge what's good or not, working or not working—just let it be. Use your heart's love to intuit abundant love in your mind room. When your mind is at peace and in a loving mood, it feels good. A good mood fuels good moves in benefiting you and those around you.
- ❖ Imagine your heart centre as a beautiful fragrant rosebud that is just about to start opening. The most exquisite and perfect rose—that is who you eternally are. Allow your beauty to unfold; give yourself permission to revel in your true inner beauty. Watch the true *You* opening up, petal by petal, as you release the purity and fragrance of your essence. Do not be surprised at accessing your true beauty, your self-worth. Every time you do this exercise, be open to what your Inner Being blesses you with. Journal your experiences, the better to be refreshed by them whenever you read and re-read how your heart centre enriches you—from deep within.

3) Wealth

The road to prosperity for many is their *desire* to acquire wealth. As the "Money Lady" Suze Orman points out, *"Money has no power of its own. You alone are the power source."* You alone set into motion waves of energy that generate wealth and abundance.

Yet, wealth is more than just acquiring financial wealth. True wealth is embracing the larger universe of good physical health, loving relationships that nurture mind and heart, an understanding family, a harmonious workplace and a safe neighbourhood to live in.

How could a person be wealthy if they lacked good health and a stable family life? Of what use would lots of money be then?

In other words, you set into motion frequencies and vibrations that attract wealth, abundance and prosperity to enrich your life. The stronger your desires, the more potent the results. That is not to say you'll just wish upon a star and loll around doing nothing.

Rather, the **intensity of your aspirations** to acquire wealth broadcasts itself to the universe—the more intense your desires, the farther afield your messages resonate, and the more opportunities arise to meet and fulfil your desires.

When you tune in to these opportunities (instead of doubting and suspecting them with your mind when they present themselves to you) and listen with your heart, you'll find yourself gaining huge grounds on business leads and expanding your business contacts with neuroscience.

For example, as a businessperson, you cannot afford to miss out on another avenue for prospecting leads—by using your heart's light! How does this work? People buy from people they trust intuitively and wordlessly.

When people feel your sincerity in wanting to offer them the best, their hearts feel your honest intentions too, and a lifelong connection is made. For businesses to stay competitive, it only makes sense to sustain limited resources by reselling to repeat customers—instead of spinning your wheels to attract new leads to generate sales.

As I keep reiterating, there is a higher force in all of us—the soul. When you offer your soul's love, integrity and respect to everyone you meet, only good things happen with positive heart-to-heart exchanges.

Finally, a really important realisation is the inverse relation between earning money and accumulating it, and in giving back. For example, the more experienced you become, the more you can charge for your services. When some people reach this point in their lives, the motivation to work harder and to keep growing diminishes. It's like—"I've done what's needed."

But, everyone quickly learns that complacency is the antidote to making progress on Life's highway. No one can get joy from giving less to every endeavour they pursue.

Therefore, you have the responsibility to continuously expand your vision, to keep on evolving as a divine being—and contributing back to society all the more.

EXERCISE: STRETCHING & REACHING TO WEALTH

- ASK: What can I do every day to stretch my talent in growing a little more? If I'm a human resource manager, can I process 5-10 extra job resumes every day? Bottom line—it does make you feel good in filling positions that need filling, even as you're helping move people off joblessness back into productive jobs. This is personal enrichment that is win-win-win—for you, prospective hirees and your company.
- ASK: What would I like to leave as my legacy to family and community? How do I make the world a more loving and kinder place? Do I notice how my tone of voice can be an instrument of good will and my gentle words in healing a strained atmosphere?
- ASK: How do I show by my actions that I invite abundance into my world? How can I be more generous with my time, energy, good will, help and willingness to take on extra projects at work and at home—without any thought of extra compensation?
- ASK: How do I inspire others to feel good about giving more of themselves, too? TIP: Remember, actions speak louder than words. We inspire others, even as they inspire us, wordlessly.

Chapter 4.

THREE HUMAN LIMITATIONS TO OVERCOME – F.E.A.R or (FALSE EVIDENCE APPEARING REAL) DOUBT & INSECURITY

> ***Deepen your faith in yourself.***
> ***Nothing will be able to frighten***
> ***Or weaken you.***
> ***~ Sri Chinmoy***

Just as we honour three dominant desires for love, health and wealth in getting ahead with our lives, we have to recognize that it's human nature to have to deal with three dominant limitations that hold us back in our personal development, too.

Fear, doubt and insecurity weigh us down with negative energy. If you succumb to them, or even cherish them unknowingly, you do yourself a disservice because you're attracting more of the same negative energy to pull you down even more.

I'll explain and show you how simple it is to disable negative and uncomely fear, doubt and insecurity from your consciousness and thereafter, to keep on making progress with your newfound ***confidence* and *courage***—by invoking your true potential from within!

1) F.E.A.R. or False Evidence Appearing Real

It's revealing that the acronym for "False Evidence Appearing Real" is an old foe—FEAR.

You've experienced fear brought on by a "fight or flight" response. For example, getting lost late at night and almost running out of petrol in your car. This, however, is merely an acute feeling of panic and fear that is temporary. After regaining your bearings, it's all over and -phew!- you're back on to a steady course again.

However, there are people who are chronically fearful—of not being able to deal with themselves and with others. They even fear themselves! They fear the past, the present and the future. They fear their friends and enemies. They are fearful of everything and everybody. They have a chronic fear of failure and paradoxically, even fear of success.

Fear as a negative energy has a powerful source—vital energy. That is why understanding the source and causes of fear is fundamental in letting go of f.e.a.r.

As I've discussed earlier, your vital energy is double-edged (like the other energies of the heart, mind and physical). You can either use your vital energy as a positive force by being courageous and confident to invite success and progress into your life—or allow the obverse negative aspects to cripple you as a debilitating energy manifesting as f.e.a.r.

But, fear not! We *can* overcome fear and expel f.e.a.r! Let's begin by examining some causes and reasons for unrealistic fear in our lives.

1 Fear of failure. For anyone, be they student or business owner, the fear of failure is a major cause for failure in of itself. How come? As we've mentioned often, the Law of Attraction will heap those who are insecure about succeeding with more of the same. Sri Chinmoy explains in *The Divine Hero: Winning in the Battlefield of Life* (Watkins, 2002), *"The very idea of a mistake being shameful or unmentionable creates a wrong vibration in the cosmos. First, let us take mistakes as failures. What are failures? They are the pillars of success. Second, let us take mistakes as half-truths ... then we can see in them an iota of truth, then we can feel that the mistakes can be rectified or transformed into truth."* How encouraging and simple it is! Just switch from thinking on a negative wavelength to a positive one. Just do it, whenever you catch yourself thinking fearful thoughts!

2 Fear of what others think. Why should you be spending time thinking about what others think? All that energy is better used towards your own self-discovery. If you're fearful of

losing friends who don't understand why you're showing the courage of conviction to be true to yourself, may I suggest you're better off without them? Meditate, pray and affirm your positive intentions instead of allowing others to dictate a miserable existence for you! Allow your true potential to shine forth—while wordlessly inspiring these people to seek within themselves, too. Now, this elevates personal development into a sacred service because you're giving others permission to come into their own potential, as well. Isn't this a powerful and life-changing realisation? You're actually helping yourself and others to alter your previous hapless situations by steering into a new life course blessed with infinite possibilities!!

3 <u>Fear of the finite.</u> Instead of worrying about yesterday, today or tomorrow, focus your thoughts and energy on the *IN*FINITE POWER OF YOUR SOUL. Access this immortal resource to provide inspiration and solutions. Spend time reflecting and meditating for guidance from within to guide and protect your actions on the outer plane. When you acknowledge that you're of and from a higher power, your Creator, you'll finally enjoy the fruits of self-discovery. How so? Because your Creator created you for the purpose of playing with and enjoying His Cosmic Play—by identifying with His True Wealth in becoming one with the Universe.

See how unreasonable it is to open up your precious being to negative energy supporting "false evidence appearing real—f.e.a.r."?

EXERCISE: EXPELLING F.E.A.R.!!

- ASK: What makes me fearful—my own qualities, other people, situations, events, the weather, fear of flying, etc.?
- List each one on a note card. Turn the card (or piece of paper) over and write down the obverse positive qualities.
- Shuffle the cards and stack them in a pile.
- Pick out one card. See what that f.e.a.r is. Then say, "I'm expelling my fear of my mum-in-law! NOW!!" On the other side of the card you would have written down her positive qualities such as—"she brings us the most yummy homemade pie every time she visits" or "she's our reliable babysitter whenever we need her." Don't even think of her nagging, complaining ways and what a drag she can be! Start appreciating her *good* qualities—and they'll come to touch you silently and positively. You'll both start enjoying each other on a better headspace. Inevitably, you set in motion a chain of positive emotional changes that will wordlessly morph into appreciation springing forth from both sides. That is the idea—healing a rift with good intentions!
- Do this with every f.e.a.r. you've written out. Castigate a negative quality that has been festering at you and preventing you from manifesting your courage and bravery.
- Schedule this as a daily ritual for personal growth.
- Consciously remind yourself why you need to release f.e.a.r. ("false evidence appearing real!") every time you're intimidated or assailed by f.e.a.r. Tell yourself how much more constructive it is to use negative energy for positive gains—and springboard on to boundless, unhorizoned and glorious opportunities!!

Knowing your ability to consciously radiate positive health, strength and harmony will bring you to the realisation that there is nothing to fear—because you're constantly in touch with Infinite Strength from The Source.

Here's how one spiritual master explains why the obverse of fear is hope. When Sri Chinmoy gave a lecture at the University of Edinburgh in 1974 (*My Rose Petals, Part 3*), he explains, "*What is hope? Hope is man's preparation for the unknown.*

Hope is man's inner effort. An ordinary man is not aware of this inner effort, but a seeker of the highest Truth is fully aware of it. This inner effort inspires the seeker to see something new, to feel something new, to say something new, to do something new and, finally, to become something new.

Hope is newness. In this newness is our self-transcendence."

See how easy it is to remove f.e.a.r. by consciously shifting your focus to positive intentions and feelings such as hope, optimism, confidence, joy and determination to making progress with your life?

Instead of cherishing fear of the unknown, welcome into your life **the beauty of the unknown**. Allow the thrill of life's unknown adventures to unfold; revel in the myriad opportunities Life is gifting you! Sally forth with your courage of conviction born of confidence!

When fear is effectively and completely destroyed, your Light will shine, clouds will disperse and you'll have discovered the true Source of power, energy and Life to reinvigorate you anew!!

Mistake-making is the cosmic wisdom's way of teaching each of us how to carry on.

~ Buckminster Fuller

2) Doubt

Related to fear is the uncomely notion of doubt. It's alright to question someone or doubt something in the newspaper with a healthy dose of scepticism. But, the greatest human failing is to doubt oneself.

Why? Because when you doubt your capabilities, you're sinking your own ship. With all your God-blessed talents waiting to blossom forth, negative self-doubt prevents you from manifesting your true, unbridled potential. You can doubt others, but never ever doubt yourself and what you can do and contribute to yourself, for others, the community and back to the Universe!

The reasoning mind has to be transformed into a dedicated divine instrument to manifest all the gifts it came into the world with. That is why you need to honour your souls' light to transform uncomely qualities into manifesting true divinity.

3) Insecurity

Another ugly cousin of fear and doubt is—insecurity. Can you see how intertwined they are in strangling your good intentions and starving your divine talents from manifesting your potential?

Again, instead of allowing them to overwhelm and overpower you, identify with the true power of your soul's light from within.

Focus intensely on positive opposites. Meditate on and affirm your heroism for the courage of your convictions to carry on during the day, by giving your best at every moment.

Certainly, there's no insecurity when you block it out—by focusing on and being committed to getting good results, is there? Again, like attracts like; positive aspirations *will* transform unholy thoughts.

Successfully invoke your valour to snuff out self-doubt. Insist with your heart's sincere intensity to visualise and affirm your self-worth. No one can do this for you. **You have to want it enough to do it yourself.**

Start empowering your mindset with your heartfelt convictions. Allow the light of your soul to ignite all your senses. Be the authentic person you're born to be.

Live your own reality with your understated and powerful presence that everyone can feel when you walk into a room!

When you feel your true inner strength emerging, don't be intimidated by it. Revel in your own True Power. Love and enjoy the fact that you're finally able to access your true potential—and giving back unalloyed Joy, Love and Gratitude to the Universe.

We see so many powerful women and men who have come into their own and are confident in having discovered their unique powers: U.S. President Barack and Mrs. Michelle Obama, Oprah, Suze Orman, Donna Brazile and Dr. Shirley Ann Jackson that I've mentioned earlier on are but a few who show determination in overcoming their initial perceived limitations.

The opposite can also happen when other people become jealous of your success and popularity—just as you're trying your hardest to override other people's negativity. Don't let frustration and jealousy stop you from realising your true potential.

For example, when U.S. President Barack Obama was awarded the Nobel Peace Prize, you'd think Americans would be happy and proud and indeed, many are. But, ironically, the greatest acclaim came from overseas. Sadly, many Americans are mired in negative situations of joblessness, depressing financial market situations and housing foreclosures. It became prime time for opposing Republican Party members to attack the president.

Luckily though, this president and his wife are strong and stalwart champions who want to pursue good intentions for their country and the whole world. Other people do sense and feel it—when some people try to override unwarranted criticisms.

That is what you'll do, too, when you:

1 **Accept** that f.e.a.r is an unreal force preventing you from achieving your life goals and dreams

2 **Transform** f.e.a.r. into New Hope by throwing out fear of the unknown. Instead, you're focusing on the New Beauty of the Unknown filled with hopeful accomplishments to enrich your life with endless possibilities that the Universe is waiting to gift you—if you but open your heart to receiving them with confidence and abiding faith!!

3 **Illumine** f.e.a.r. with the power of your soul's light. When you finally know that this acronym stands for "false evidence appearing real," you'll understand how easy it is to cast it off your mental-vital makeup of unnecessary fear.

4 **Transcend the impossible** by donning your armour of bravery and the courage of your convictions—by identifying with The Real in You to overcome seemingly impossible odds! You are of The Source—Powerful and Invincible!

YOU can do all of this—by being determined to strip away your perceived emotional and mental bondage and limitations. I'm always eager to hear from you about your progress; please send emails to: felicity@felicityokolo.com

When we finally realise we're of The Source, we'll see how debilitating it's been to harbour anything less than the very best of our spiritual aspirations!

We can think of no better symbol of man's earthly life than that of the seed planted in the darkness of the earth in order that it may grow into the perfect flower. The perfect flower, the archetypal flower, is created first in the mind of God, and then the seed is planted in the earth to grow to fullness. So it is with you, who are as seeds planted in physical form to grow towards the light until you become perfect sons and daughters of God—the perfect archetypal God-man which God held in His mind in the beginning.

~ White Eagle in *Spiritual Unfoldment1: How to Discover the Invisible Worlds and Find the Source of Healing,* 1961 (from *The Road Within*, edited by Sean O'Reilly, James O'Reilly & Tim O'Reilly)

Chapter 5.

PERSONAL DEVELOPMENT APPLICATIONS

Make it thy business to know thyself, which is the most difficult lesson in the world.

~ Miguel de Cervantes

Let's do a quick review of some personal development applications you can confidently tackle with the plethora of techniques for self-discovery we've covered.

Questions

When you require information on whatever you need to know, you have online search engines to get instant answers from, such as Google and YouTube.

However, the next step would be to ask, what should I do? How much information do I really need to begin my quest to become a happier person? How do I know enough is enough, or not enough?

Asking the right questions and asking better questions will result in right answers and better answers and this is achieved when you ask empowering questions by using "what" instead of "why." It seems that we have been programmed to seek to understand a situation and that is why we ask WHY. "Why" questions are good for getting information if you are doing research or exploration of some kind and similar activities. But they are not good when you want solution to a problem or challenge. "Why" questions are not empowering but WHAT questions are the right kinds of questions to ask and they are very empowering. While WHY questions tend to go round the challenge or problem and tend to search for someone or something to blame, WHAT questions are targeted to give clarity about the problem or challenge and tend to search for solution. Examples of WHY questions are "WHY am I not succeeding?" A WHAT version will be "WHAT will make me successful?" Instead of asking, " Why am failing?" ask, " What will get me what I want?" Instead of asking, "Why can't I get this?" ask, "What do I need to know to understand?" For more empowering questions and other resources for you to download to help you further, visit www.felicityokolo.com on Free Resources page or email: felicity@felicityokolo.com

By asking empowering questions, your brain begins to work to help and support you. You are also asking the Universe to help and support you. It's that simple. You only have to set aside quiet time and the effort to question and dialog. If you can spend hours on the phone talking with someone else, why can't you allow yourself permission to dialog with the Universe and your Inner Self?

That is when your spiritual depth comes to your aid, by using some of these techniques:

- Personal meditation. When you connect with the light of your soul during meditation, you'll intuitively feel and know the answers. Enter your meditative quest not with a demand, but with a humble request to do what's right by the Universe. Meditation is silence, to better hear the cosmic answers specially meant for you.
- Prayerful requests. When we pray with soulful intensity for answers, they are bound to come. Prayer is talking to a higher power. Meditation is listening to answers.
- Bird of Aspiration. That is when your soul bird flies with both aspiration wings—prayer and meditation wings. You need both wings to soar in your quest for personal growth and development.
- Affirmation or mantra. In India, soulful chanting is a divine invocation to invoke the Highest to bless and guide your life. It's not a mechanical repetition of a keyword or phrase. Rather, an affirmation is a soulful repetition that reverberates from the very depths of your being. As such, a powerful mantra can illumine and transform into the very essence of the quality you're invoking.

That is where quantum physics chimes in by describing your intense aspiration as magnetic reverberations and frequencies to attract "like" energy with the Law of Attraction. Allow the sincere intensity of your seeking to supply the answers from within you.

Ultimately, you'll find that YOU are The Source of all answers to your questions! You only have to dig deeper with your questions.

> **The beautiful thing about the law of attraction is that you can begin where you are, and you can begin to think, "real thinking," and you can begin to generate within yourself a feeling tone of harmony and happiness. The law will begin to respond to that.**
>
> **And you can break yourself free from your hereditary patterns, cultural codes, social beliefs and prove once and for all that the power within you is greater than the power within the world.**
>
> **~ Michael Bernard Beckwith**

Projection

We communicate our needs and desires. While communicating our intents, we project our emotions, as well. The beauty of realising the potential of your inner wealth is to be able to apply a directed and focused projection to communicate clearly in specifying your needs and desires.

Sports psychologists use mental imagery in applying it to a technique called: *projection*. When you visualise a blueprint of what you want—say, a new job overseas that allows you to travel—then you set in motion a visual process.

It's like producing a movie. You ask the Universe for guidance on a best-fit job in, for example, Australia. You'd like to combine your scuba-diving interests with exploring coral reefs that are fast disappearing—you want to see them before they become extinct, yet not want to spend too much of what you've saved, while doing it.

Begin projecting your dream on the big screen by envisioning in detail, step by step, of how you're going to do it.

1 Find a good-fit job in Sydney, Australia, that comes with relocation expenses, housing allowance and perhaps even a car.

2 If it were winter in London, you'd like to get a job that flies you down to Sydney as soon as possible, as it's summer there. Provide the Universe a specific timeline.

3 See in your mind the employment agency working smoothly with the travel agency to facilitate your trip Down Under.
4 See yourself leaving on a bleak winter night on a flight that flies you south to arrive on a bright summer morning in Sydney. Is this for real? You bet! If your projection is done with sincerity and intensity, and this is the intuitive answer that your meditation shows you to be the right action to undertake, it will happen. Don't for even one moment throw in doubt, for this negative energy will invalidate the whole process!

That is how you can use projection as a change model to alter any circumstance you're chafing under to actualise more positive outcomes.

You're communicating your wishes to the Universe:

1 Of your intention to enact changes
2 In your firm belief of these forthcoming changes, and
3 Your gratefully receiving the outcomes you've projected onto the Cosmic Screen.

The Law of Attraction is at your service with any thoughts you wish to project—for your health, wealth and ultimate happiness.

It's a pretty powerful realisation when you grasp this law, isn't it? It's even more amazing when things start happening miraculously! When you finally get into the groove of welcoming serendipity as a sweet friend, you'll know you've arrived - thanks to the Law of Attraction.

Responsibility

Along with the liberating power of realising and using your powerful energies of the mind, vital, body, heart and soul comes the responsibility of utilising them for positive purposes.

Think about how power-hungry dictators have ruined the lives and economies of millions of people—and karmic retribution impacting their future lives.

Power is indeed double-edged. Power for positive change on the individual and collective levels are needed to bring about better living conditions and it starts with your power of responsible transformation for your own personal growth, first.

After you're aware of this, then it is time to contribute back to society and the common good. You're free to act responsibly.

The catch? "Freedom" is not really a "free" privilege to use anyhow and any which way. Your soul has a mission to manifest. It's your mission to discover what it is, as it's different for everyone.

That is what makes the process of personal development such an adventure-filled journey! Relish it and enjoy the process; in many ways, the journey is as important as the destination.

To help you further, I have prepared very powerful questions for you to download at www.felicityokolo.com on Free Resources page. It will help with your progress in your journey.

When the voice and the vision on the inside become more profound, clear and loud than the opinions on the outside, you've mastered your Life!

~ Dr. John Demartini

Creativity & Purposeful Creation

Now that you're aware of your mission to discover the purpose of your life's journey, you can get creative.

Purposeful creation is attempting every project with a focused inquiry. Creativity flows because you're delving into your powerful depths to discover divinely correct ways of helping yourself and others achieve worthwhile results to improve current conditions.

That is creative energy at work—when you purposefully attempt to discover better ways (not necessarily the cheapest or a "biased best way") to build a better mousetrap.

How to create? We create with:

- Words & Affirmations
- Pictures or images we hold in our mind
- The thoughts we think

The **words** we use reflect a deeper intent from within. Even toddlers can be very forceful about, "I don't want to go!" These words communicate a deeper intent that goes beyond surface likes and dislikes. Emotions and intentions are created and amplified. Our words are very powerful and are alive. Negative or bad words are disempowering and they hurt. Knowing that your words are made up of creative forces that have the power to build or destroy makes you very powerful. When positive or good words that are empowering are used, they build and encourage rather than destroy and discourage.

Affirmations are very powerful creative words. "Affirmations are not only an ancient art, but also a modern and scientific technique. Scientists declare that the body as well as the universe is filled with innate intelligence. By taking a statement filled with good words and declaring it over and over again, you gain the conscious attention of innate intelligence that is ever active in the subconscious functions of the body—in every cell of the mind and body tissues."

If you'll recall, I've already discussed this at length in relating this innate intelligence and vibrations of the universe to neuroscience.

The **pictures or images** of ourselves that we hold in our mind are manifested in our external world as things we want. If you fill your mind with pictures or images of your current realities that you don't want, then you will keep creating similar conditions in your life. It is best to fill your mind with pictures or images of the conditions you want, to manifest those instead.

The **thoughts** we think create our world. Whatever thoughts, negative or positive, good or bad, that you think over and over again in your mind, result in their respective outcomes. We are spiritual beings and **spirit** is energy—subtle energy of the cosmos that is in every person, thing and nature. Our thoughts absorb the power of this spirit and we hold it in our inner consciousness, meld it into our ordinary consciousness and finally, manifest as creative energy and power.

This creative power is impersonal and your ability to think is your ability to control it and make use of it for the benefit of **yourself and others.** Remember, **"To know and not to do, is not yet to know**.

Create with certainty. Imagine and create. Albert Einstein observed, *"Imagination is more powerful than knowledge."*

Start imagining and creating what you want as an established fact with the Law of Attraction. That is why the freedom to create comes with the responsibility to create wisely.

When you understand **what** and **why** your reasons are in creating your life, purpose and destiny, you empower creativity to befriend your spiritual aspirations in manifesting your life's mission.

Now that you're no longer underestimating how powerful you are, start envisioning and creating a more satisfying Life with the power of the Universe to help you.

Need more proof that you are what you think you can be and do what you think you can do, with the power of your pure intentions realistically imagining positive outcomes?

Let me then end this chapter by highlighting how another person overcame the odds—simply by being *fearless* about *wanting* to make a better life for himself and the whole world.

Cesar Millan was an illegal immigrant from Mexico who trekked across the U.S.-Mexico border in 1990 with nothing in his pockets and his life hanging on a thread.

In case Cesar's name is familiar, your home may be one of 70 million across the globe with access to National Geographic Channel's weekly TV-series, "Dog Whisperer with Cesar Millan."

His fourth book, *How to Raise the Perfect Dog* was just published. The other three books are *New York Times* bestsellers and are selling in 14 countries.

How did Mr. Millan, who could hardly speak English when he arrived in California, ace his celebrity production deal and status?

As the *New York Times* reported (October 10, 2009), "Mr. Millan calls the deal, which he agreed to on instinct, a blessing. 'The goal that God and I have together is the whole world transformed through a dog. God was my lawyer,' he says. 'And so He's going to bring you great people, and those great people are going to give you your fair share without you asking.'"

Indeed, Mr. Millan is an adamant advocate of, *"Anything that is realistic, if I create it in my mind, it can become a reality,"* he says, evoking one of his favourite authors, the self-help superstar Wayne W. Dyer. **"That is the power of intention."**

Remember, it's never ever too late to start. The inspiration to begin hits different people at various times—just be thankful and celebrate the fact that you are even considering taking such a momentous step with your personal development by reading this!

There is no limit to what this law can do for you; dare to believe in your own ideal; think of the ideal as an already accomplished fact.

~ Charles Haanel

Chapter 6.

SYSTEMIC IMPACT OF BELIEFS, VALUES & RULES

> **You have to start knowing yourself so well that you begin to know other people. A piece of us is in every person we can ever meet.**
>
> **~ John D. MacDonald**

Every society tries to operate as smoothly as possible with laws, rules and regulations based on historical beliefs and values embraced and passed on through generations. Systemic controls are needed to keep law, order and safety among members of civil society.

However, times and conditions change. The impact and efficacy of laws and rules have to change as well, in order to keep up with needs.

That is where your newfound awareness of *YOUR* power comes in to help mitigate situations in your life, other people, the environment and events in civil society as needed. Actually, it's a private public service you provide with your powerful awareness.

What's that? You ask. I'm asking you to consider creating responsible situations of psycho-social change and emotional empowerment whenever your inner being instinctively nudges you.

For example, our social systems based on hereditary beliefs and socio-political values are not new. They were formed eons ago and have an integral part in keeping members of society together to function more effectively and cohesively as a collective whole. Rules were made to govern and police the citizenry.

However, rules have to be broken and constructively reformed periodically to serve the common good when new needs arise. It's not wilfully breaking rules for the sake of breaking them. No!

Rather, I'm encouraging you to be responsible in seriously introducing new ways of seeing and doing things as needs arise.

That is, with your emerging powers of empowerment, it's your divine responsibility to: 1) observe what needs doing, 2) research how to do it well, and 3) work with and inspire others to foster social change to benefit the collective good.

In other words, I'm asking you to please take a long, hard look at how you're a product of our social beliefs, values and systems, and how your beliefs and value systems ripple out on to others as well. Also how you interact with neighbours, subway commuters, shopkeepers and other service personnel such as healthcare providers and the postal carrier.

Ask: "given the beliefs, values and systems I've consciously and unconsciously made for myself, how are they serving me now? What can I do to keep reinventing them to complement the goals I've set out to achieve? Are they helping or obstructing me as I expand my vision?"

Remind yourself, too, that you'll have to revisit and revise them as your aspirations evolve. The only constant here is—change.

Even as you are a change agent unto yourself with your newfound self-discoveries, your growing awareness of your divine responsibility will inspire you to work for the common good.

That is when the ultimate prayer, "Father Thy Will Be Done," takes your spiritual aspiration up to a higher level of aspiration when you become a conscious and unconditionally surrendered instrument of the Divine.

That is when; too, divine surrender absolves you of human attachment to the results of your actions—when you embark on the high and not impossible road to positive change for your self and others.

How to transform others, you ask? Here's what 'Dog Whisperer' Cesar Millan suggests we consider:

1 World transformation begins with self-transformation

2 Don't judge others

3 Live in the present, the eternal now

4 Maintain your personal and emotional balance by remaining calm and assertive (cool, calm, easy does it!)

5 Be realistic about what you can create for yourself and for others—then do it!

6 A dog, man's best friend, is an ever ready ally "to transform the moment" because animals do understand themselves, you and the environment intuitively

7 Your fluid and relaxed movements communicate authenticity and confidence more than words can

8 When you come into your own, everyone feels Your Power—from animals to the entire planet of humanity!

9 When you communicate power and confidence, you command *respect* wherever you go, regardless of the fact that you were born dirt-poor, as Cesar Millan was

10 When you enter a room, smile and offer, "What can I do to help?" Be the transforming change agent that you are by emanating the balanced energy field you access from within—to transform irrational fears in others!

When you get a chance to watch "Dog Whisperer" (either from a DVD or TV show), you'll see that here's someone who walks the talk—as everyone should.

You'll finally know and understand your origin as a spiritual being with unlimited powers. And, start letting go of F.E.A.R. by keeping your head high and both feet on the ground—no matter what happens!

Imagine, too, the transformational powers you inspire others to undertake. When that happens, POWER expands exponentially! As anthropologist Margaret Mead noted, and is often quoted on, *"Never doubt that a small group of thoughtful, committed citizens can change the world; indeed, it's the only thing that ever has."*

Margaret Mead also advised, ***"Always remember that you are absolutely unique. Just like everyone else."***

Our uniqueness and power which we inherited from our maker is innate and in every one of us. Just like in the story of the littlest god, after all avenues have been explored by the other gods, then the Littlest God, who had been silent until then, spoke up.

"Why don't we hide these resources inside each human being? They'll never think to look for them there!"

Chapter 7.

LIVING AS SPIRITUAL BEINGS BY USING OUR INTUITION

Exert your talents, and distinguish yourself, and don't think of retiring from the world, until the world will be sorry that you retire.

~ Samuel Johnson

We must learn to live by what we love. To know and understand yourself is to know and understand that you are a spiritual being–a god. Knowing you are godlike because you are of God means living in a godlike mode that you truly are. Since God is love, why settle for less? Why play small? Why expect anything less?

Thus, to live godlike is to live in divinity. You're not doing yourself or others any favour by not living up to your god potential.

Living less like the god that you are means living at a subsistence level as a human being. In this human mode, your focus is on basic survival–constantly trying to survive like a peasant instead of living fully in what you love doing, such as creating abundance and enjoying it.

When you live in your birthright, your divinity, you're more intuitive. This means cultivating a life connected to your heart and soul. You're happy because there's no compromise on what you love and you're not settling for less.

Living this way enables you to excel and create wealth, build happy relationships with family, friends, and businesses and contribute to the world because you love doing it, not because you have to.

On the other hand, when you live based on your basic level of human subsistence, you use your belief systems in reacting to wanton thoughts and feelings dictated by mental constraints. Living at this lower level means operating in survival humanity mode.

People believe they have to make a living to survive before doing what they love. On the contrary, the opposite is true. You do what you love in creating the lifestyle you want–beyond your wildest dreams.

Great leaders and successful entrepreneurs do what they love to be successful, and not the other way round. Some tried living in their humanity mode but got frustrated. As soon as they switched and went with their hearts in doing what they loved, there was a massive transformation in their personal and business life.

Examples are Walt Disney of Disney Land, Richard Branson of Virgin Group and JK Rowling of the *Harry Potter* series. They did not become an overnight success. JK Rowling said it took her ten years to become an overnight success. No one says it'll be a smooth ride but you must persist and persevere because the reward is far greater than living in a humanity mode of basic survival.

The reason it seems difficult in the beginning and that it takes longer to be highly successful is because of the tremendous effort you'd have to make to unlearn old ways of looking at the world. Albert Einstein observed, *"We cannot solve our problems with the same thinking we used when we created them."*

Like JK Rowling, many people have to reach a low, low stage in their lives before deciding that it's no use living the way they did. They simply forgot to live like the god they are. They started realising there has to be a better way of rebuilding their lives. And thus began their inner seeking and introspection by tuning in to the voice of intuition.

These life patterns are perpetually depicted in movies. *The Matrix, Star Wars* and *Harry Potter* show how the hero is unaware of their birthright and live less than a god, and live peasant-like, until their lives are threatened. That is when they start seeking more in-depth answers to their current life situations.

The script is one where the hero is called to adventure by following their heart in doing what they love (which could lead them through the unknown), or stay where they are (in conditions known to them). If the hero decides to go with what they love as many do, they meet a wise person who helps them on the journey and trains them to meet headlong a plethora of unknowns along their questing trail. The hero at this stage can choose to refuse the call and regress back to living like peasant - less than their divinity.

The hero next faces their demons that come from a fear of transitioning from humanity mode to divinity mode and 'dies.' After the death of their humanity mode, they resurrect to a new life–in finding their inner wealth; that is, they become aware and understand their divinity; and start living a new life based on what they love and honour.

This phase is quite magical with the hero putting into service their divinity to serve others by contributing, by making a difference and training other seekers called to adventure like them.

Whatever the phase of your journey that you're in right now is irrelevant. What's important is to know and understand what's happening, why you're seeking, who you are and what you love.

You must realise that your thoughts and feelings are much louder than your intuition–the 'little voice'- and that your intuition leads you to the true perspective of your inborn divinity, where intuition enables you to engage your potential in creating what you love.

You have to learn how to lower the volume of your thoughts and feelings and to start increasing the volume of your heartfelt intuition; followed by welcoming intuition to play its rightful role in placing it in the forefront of your consciousness.

Why do I stress this? Because acknowledging your intuition is inherent with your divinity, and you'll notice your thoughts and feelings are less real because they were formed from societal and historical beliefs programmed since childhood.

Your thoughts and feelings inform your perception of reality, not your soul's true reality. Thoughts keep changing. Truth however, remains *the* truth–no matter your outer circumstances. Being divine means we're connected to one another and everything–as opposed to living in humanity mode where we feel separated from everything, especially our birthright's true divinity.

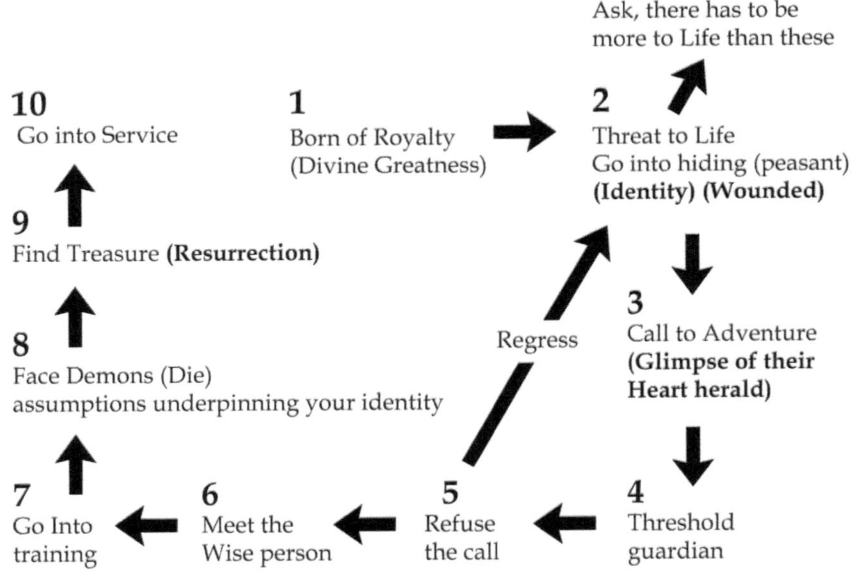

To start living in your divinity regardless of outer circumstances, ask yourself:

What do I love?

What is my divinity?

What are my inherent gifts?

What is the true power within me that I want to manifest and contribute to the world?

What legacy do I want to leave?

How can I help others come to their divinity?

Knowing some answers to the above questions will help you begin to live life based on love, truth and service, as your intuition gifts you infinite possibilities in creating a fresh new life. Love is where it all starts and continues. Truth supports love, where your intuition leads you to love. Intuition puts you to service–to serve with love by tapping into your infinite wisdom.

3 Core Values

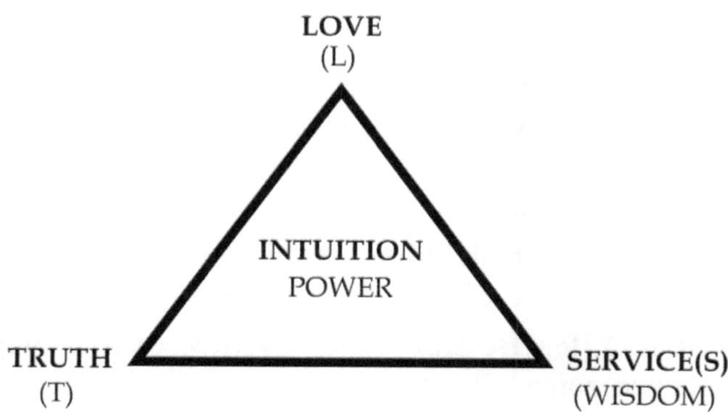

How To Access Your Intuition At Will

Accessing your intuition keeps you in control of your life, leaves you with infinite options and helps with better decision-making.

TO DO: How To Access Your Intuition At Will (Exercise)

You can access your intuition at will using the following steps:

1 Close your eyes and take a deep breathe. Exhale slowly and feel your body relaxing. **Acknowledge your thoughts and feelings**, notice the tension they are creating within you and do nothing about them.

2 **Choose to be Innocent**. Imagine stepping into innocence–the unknown, where everything is just, as is. By making this choice, you're choosing to step into your intuitive wisdom.

3 **Choose to be of Service**. Choose to serve your divinity with love and truth. Imagine a rich golden circle surrounds you. Imagine that you are connected with your divinity.

4 **Imagine the End Result**. Use your imagination and engage it in the end result of your divinity.

5 **Receive a symbol.** Once connected with your imagination, ask for a symbol to emerge to inform you of your divinity.

6 **Observe what's obvious of the symbol and make it up**. Open your eyes and describe the symbol and interpret it in relation to your divinity and keep making it up and as you do, so it begins to ring true.

The state of Innocence in the exercise above has three qualities:

- **Your ability to not know** (which enables you to step into the Divine where your intuition exists).
- **Realize that everything is made up.** (Your God given ability is the ability to make things up. Do not be fixed on HOW it should be or how it is known to be, just MAKE IT UP.)
- **To be in Life**. (Be surrounded by flow of life. Step into the innocence zones where you see magic and majesty in things and appreciate people more.)

The true purpose of intuition is to serve your divinity. It reveals the truth of who you really are, helps you know yourself and facilitates your ability to know what you can create in your divinity. You must recognise that knowing yourself is the gateway to having all you want in life.

Your Focus

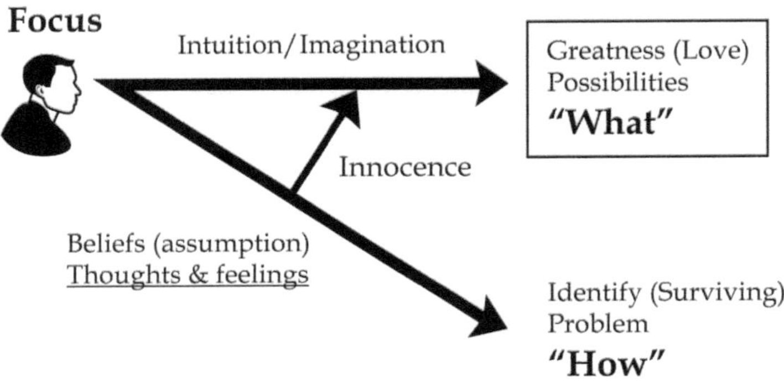

Whatever you focus on in life will create results accordingly. Focusing on your humanity mode means focusing on the basics of survival with end results based on limited beliefs. On the other hand, focusing on your divinity means focusing on end results (on WHAT you love without the HOW) using your intuition and imagination to create endless possibilities.

What results are you producing in your life right now? What is the reality most apparent? Whatever the reality is right now will let you know what you have been focused or focusing on; in other words, your reality reveals your focus. If you are not happy with the reality, just change your focus.

Your Intuition comes to the rescue in decision-making or when trying to resolve a problem or conflict.

The following exercise is useful to tune in to your intuition to help you make better decisions and to resolve problems or conflicts.

TO DO: Decision-Making, Problem or Conflict to Resolve

Part 1: Decision-Making, Problem or Conflict to Resolve In Your Humanity

1 What decision do you want to make or problem/conflict do you wish to resolve? State it

2 What are you thinking about the decision or conflict?

3 What are you feeling about the decision or conflict?

4 How are you defining?

   a. Yourself

   b. Others

   c. The World

5 What beliefs are obvious to you?

6 What do you believe you need to do to make the decision or resolve the Conflict/problem? (That is, what strategies do you go into to resolve the tension?)

7 What reality does this create?

Part 2: Creating What You Love with Your Imagination

1 What would you love in relation to your decision or conflict?

2 What obvious action is there to take to have what you'd love?

Part 3: Tune into What You Love with Your Intuition

1 Acknowledge Your Thoughts & Feelings
2 Choose to be in Innocence (In the unknown, the mystery)
3 Imagine the end result of what you love
4 Choose to receive a symbol that will inform you of what you love.
5 Observe what's obvious about what you love and make it up until it rings true.
6 What will it lead to if you take action on what rings true?

Living your life based on your beliefs (humanity mode) or based on your intuition/imagination (divinity/greatness mode) results in a belief cycle or imagination cycle.

The Belief Cycle is also called the Reactive Cycle and the Imagination Cycle also called the Proactive Cycle.

Belief or Reactive Cycle

In this cycle you are constantly trying to resolve issues.

1 You go into action and your **belief gets triggered**, creating tension. This tension needs resolving.
2 You try to resolve this tension with your **thoughts and feelings** creating further tension.
3 This new tension you try to resolve with **belief strategies,** using these strategies in fact create more tension instead of decreasing tension.
4 With all this tension created you end up **creating a problem.** As a result of creating this problem you end up having more thoughts and feelings and these thoughts and feelings end up **triggering more beliefs** going back to stage 1.

To get out of this Reactive Cycle, imagine the end result of what you love and focus on that.

Belief Cycle/Reactive Cycle

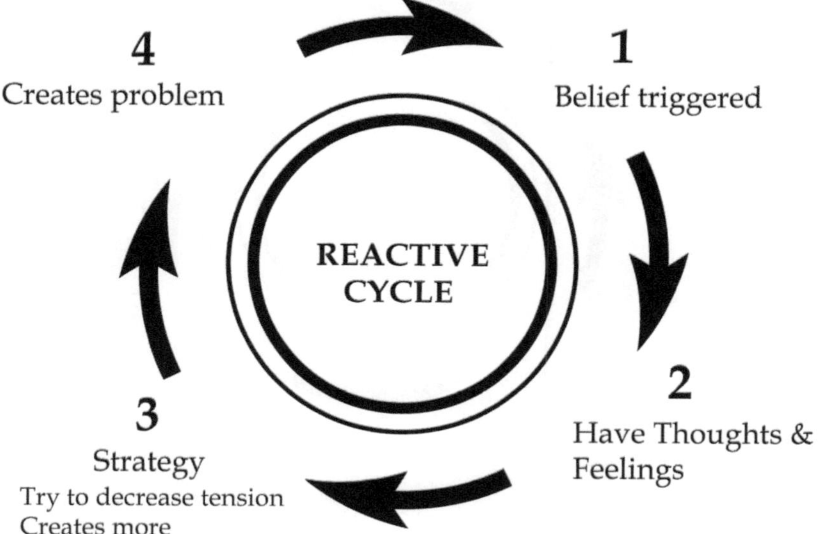

Imagination or Proactive Cycle

In this cycle you are more in control.

1 **Imagine the end result** of what you love. This increases tension.

2 You **take obvious action** towards getting what you love.

3 **End result** of what you imagined is created (or not). If what you created at this stage is not what you imagined, then you did not focus properly.

4 **Celebrate (or Re-focus).** If what you created in stage three is what you imagined then you celebrate your success and go to stage 1 to begin a new process on something different, if it is not you re-focus and go back to stage 1 and go through the process until you get what you want the end result to be.

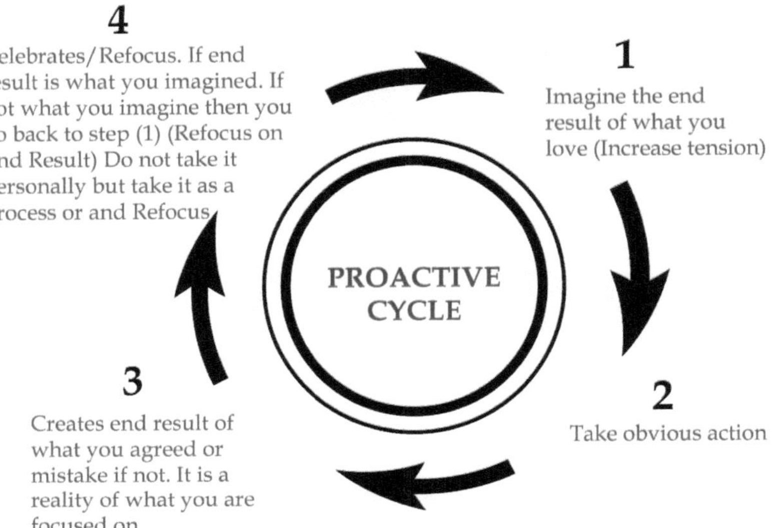

TO DO: Exercise To tune into Your Vision, Your Current Reality and Bridge (bridge here is what needs to be done to get you from your current reality to your Vision)

1 Do How To Access Your Intuition At Will Exercise steps 1-6 for your **Vision.** Tune into something your divinity/greatness would love, you could use the symbol for previous exercise if you wish, tune into the end result)

2 Do How To Access Your Intuition At Will Exercise steps 1-6 for your **Current Reality (this is where you are at the moment in you life).** Tune into it and see what your beliefs and strategies are doing to your plans.

3 Do How To Access Your Intuition At Will Exercise steps 1-6 for the **Bridge.** Tune into something your divinity/greatness would love, you could use the symbol for previous exercise if you wish, tune into the end result and ask for a symbol to emerge that will reveal the bridge – what steps are necessary for you to take to achieve your vision.)

4 Choose the vision and choose to act on the bridge by saying "I choose to take the vision "….." (state the end result of vision) and choose to act on the bridge "….." (State the bridge) to get to the end result "…" (State end result)"

If unclear of vision or bridge, re-focus and re-do the exercise and put the bridge as the goal/end result and start again and keep questioning.

To retain and continue living in your divinity, frequently keep tuning in by using the 6-step process to access your intuition at will.

~~~

XOXO

~~~

May I be at peace.
May my heart remain open.
May I know the beauty of my true nature.
May I be healed.
May I be a source of healing in the world.

~ The Buddha

How we remember, what we remember, and why we remember form the most personal map of our individuality.

~ Christina Baldwin

References

Byrne, Rhonda. *The Secret*. New York, Atria Books. 2006.

Carpenter, William B. *Principles of Mental Physiology, with Their Applications to the Training and Discipline of the Mind and the Study of Its Morbid Conditions*. New York, D. Appleton. 1875.

Chinmoy, Sri. *The Divine Hero: Winning in the Battlefield of Life*. London, Watkins Publishing. 2002.

Chinmoy, Sri. *My Rose Petals, Part 3*. New York, Aum Publications. 1974.

Cover, Stephen R. *The 7 Habits of Highly Effective Families*. New York, Golden Books. 1997.

Goleman, Daniel. *Emotional Intelligence*. New York, Bantam Dell. 1995.

Hill, Napoleon. *Law of Success*. 1928. Reprinted. Arden, N.C., High Roads Media. 2004.

Kaufer, Nelly & Carol Osmer Newhouse. *A Woman's Guide to Spiritual Renewal*. New York, HarperCollins. 1994.

Kelly, Karen. *The Secret of "The Secret": Unlocking the Mysteries of the Runaway Bestseller*. New York, St. Martin's Press. 2007.

Kingsolver, Barbara. *High Tide in Tucson: Essays from Now or Never*. New York, HarperCollins. 1995.

Millan, Cesar. *New York Times*. October 11, 2009. "Whispering to Dogs and C.E.O.'s" by Amy Wallace.

Millan, Cesar & Melissa Jo Peltier. *How to Raise the Perfect Dog*. New York, Crown Books. 2009.

O, The Oprah Magazine. "The Power Issue." September 2009.

O'Reilly, Sean, James O'Reilly & Tim O'Reilly. *The Road Within*. San Francisco, Travelers' Tales. 2002.

Obama, Michelle. *Children's Health Magazine*. "She's a Mom First" by Peter Moore. November 2009.

Oliver, Jamie. *New York Times Magazine*, October 11, 2009. "Jamie Oliver Puts America's Diet on a Diet" by Alex Witchel.

Ornish, Dean. *Love and Survival*. New York, HarperCollins. 1998.

Someya, Yuki. *Time*, October 5, 2009. "Turning Japan's Used Cooking Oil into Clean Fuel" by Yuki Oda.

Wattles, Wallace. *The Science of Getting Rich*. 1910. Reprinted, Rockford, Illinois, BN Publishing. 2006.

~~~
~~~

About The Author

Felicity Okolo like each of us has been on her own journey of discovery, which she shares through her work.

She is one of the UK's leading Life Coach & Speaker especially on Women Empowerment.

Her purpose in life is to "Empower and lead people in a dynamic and passionate manner to live to their true potential all happy, healthy, prosperous, expressing love and peace for the highest good of all concerned."

www.ingramcontent.com/pod-product-compliance
Ingram Content Group UK Ltd.
Pitfield, Milton Keynes, MK11 3LW, UK
UKHW041933190726
13854UKWH00004B/1572

9 781446 162842